CHINA'S MARITIME AND OTHER GEOGRAPHIC THREATS

HEARING

BEFORE THE

SUBCOMMITTEE ON EUROPE, EURASIA, AND EMERGING THREATS

OF THE

COMMITTEE ON FOREIGN AFFAIRS HOUSE OF REPRESENTATIVES

ONE HUNDRED THIRTEENTH CONGRESS

FIRST SESSION

OCTOBER 30, 2013

Serial No. 113–103

Printed for the use of the Committee on Foreign Affairs

Available via the World Wide Web: http://www.foreignaffairs.house.gov/ or
http://www.gpo.gov/fdsys/

U.S. GOVERNMENT PRINTING OFFICE

85–315PDF   WASHINGTON : 2014

For sale by the Superintendent of Documents, U.S. Government Printing Office
Internet: bookstore.gpo.gov Phone: toll free (866) 512–1800; DC area (202) 512–1800
Fax: (202) 512–2104 Mail: Stop IDCC, Washington, DC 20402–0001

COMMITTEE ON FOREIGN AFFAIRS

EDWARD R. ROYCE, California, *Chairman*

CHRISTOPHER H. SMITH, New Jersey
ILEANA ROS-LEHTINEN, Florida
DANA ROHRABACHER, California
STEVE CHABOT, Ohio
JOE WILSON, South Carolina
MICHAEL T. McCAUL, Texas
TED POE, Texas
MATT SALMON, Arizona
TOM MARINO, Pennsylvania
JEFF DUNCAN, South Carolina
ADAM KINZINGER, Illinois
MO BROOKS, Alabama
TOM COTTON, Arkansas
PAUL COOK, California
GEORGE HOLDING, North Carolina
RANDY K. WEBER SR., Texas
SCOTT PERRY, Pennsylvania
STEVE STOCKMAN, Texas
RON DeSANTIS, Florida
TREY RADEL, Florida
DOUG COLLINS, Georgia
MARK MEADOWS, North Carolina
TED S. YOHO, Florida
LUKE MESSER, Indiana

ELIOT L. ENGEL, New York
ENI F.H. FALEOMAVAEGA, American
  Samoa
BRAD SHERMAN, California
GREGORY W. MEEKS, New York
ALBIO SIRES, New Jersey
GERALD E. CONNOLLY, Virginia
THEODORE E. DEUTCH, Florida
BRIAN HIGGINS, New York
KAREN BASS, California
WILLIAM KEATING, Massachusetts
DAVID CICILLINE, Rhode Island
ALAN GRAYSON, Florida
JUAN VARGAS, California
BRADLEY S. SCHNEIDER, Illinois
JOSEPH P. KENNEDY III, Massachusetts
AMI BERA, California
ALAN S. LOWENTHAL, California
GRACE MENG, New York
LOIS FRANKEL, Florida
TULSI GABBARD, Hawaii
JOAQUIN CASTRO, Texas

AMY PORTER, *Chief of Staff*   THOMAS SHEEHY, *Staff Director*
JASON STEINBAUM, *Democratic Staff Director*

_____

SUBCOMMITTEE ON EUROPE, EURASIA, AND EMERGING THREATS

DANA ROHRABACHER, California, *Chairman*

TED POE, Texas
TOM MARINO, Pennsylvania
JEFF DUNCAN, South Carolina
PAUL COOK, California
GEORGE HOLDING, North Carolina
STEVE STOCKMAN, Texas

WILLIAM KEATING, Massachusetts
GREGORY W. MEEKS, New York
ALBIO SIRES, New Jersey
BRIAN HIGGINS, New York
ALAN S. LOWENTHAL, California

CONTENTS

CHINA'S MARITIME AND OTHER GEOGRAPHIC THREATS

WEDNESDAY, OCTOBER 30, 2013

HOUSE OF REPRESENTATIVES,
SUBCOMMITTEE ON EUROPE, EURASIA, AND EMERGING THREATS,
COMMITTEE ON FOREIGN AFFAIRS,
Washington, DC.

The subcommittee met, pursuant to notice, at 10 o'clock a.m., in room 2255 Rayburn House Office Building, Hon. Dana Rohrabacher (chairman of the subcommittee) presiding.

Mr. ROHRABACHER. Good morning. The hearing is convened. And I recognize myself for an opening statement. Red China—and I don't hesitate to call it Red China—is the threat of the 21st Century. Since its birth as a Communist country 64 years ago this month, untold misery has befallen the world's most populous nation. Millions were killed in establishing their Marxist-Leninist dictatorship. And millions have been killed since then, millions killed, for example, in the Cultural Revolution of 50 years ago, and in the regular repression since. Today its extravagant claims do not allow for autonomy of belief or systems unless those systems are within their own control of the dictators in Beijing. It has established a concerted effort against any religion that does not worship at the altar of Mao, be it any flavor of Buddhism, Christianity, or other faiths. The Falun Gong and the Uighurs have been singled out for special persecution.

Some perhaps believe that Mao is a harmless print on a poster or a t-shirt. In reality, Mao joins the ranks of Hitler and Stalin as the 20th Century's worst characters in butchering millions of his fellow citizens.

One of our witnesses, Steve Mosher, in his book, "Hegemon: China's Plan to Dominate Asia and the World" quotes Mao telling a stunned Khrushchev, "So what if we lose 300 million people? Our women will make up for it in a generation."

Lest one think Mao a dusty old historical anachronism, foreign policy columnist Fareed Zakaria, if I got that right, in the Washington Post October 24th, "It appears that the party is choosing older Mao methods of crackdown, public confessions, and purification campaigns." What exactly does that mean?

There are millions of prisoners of conscience today in labor camps in China according to a new report by the Center for International Media Assistance, where the National Endowment for Democracy, "China's media environment remains one of the world's most restrictive in 2012."

(1)

Crimes such as rumor mongering on the internet can land one in indefinite detention. Authorities censor and harass international reporters or deny their visa applications or renewals. Physical attacks on foreign media members are a disturbing and a growing trend. And their long reach extends overseas. One of our witnesses today, Steve Mosher, had his promising academic career in the United States as the first American social scientist allowed to carry out field work in Mao's China. It was derailed over some outspoken criticism of China some years ago.

Today we look at China's external posture toward its bordering states. That is the purpose of this hearing. But China has menaced, threatened, and even attempted to absorb its neighbors, notably Tibet and Taiwan, and has clashes with virtually every bordering state. The subcommittee will examine China's threatening maritime and territorial claims.

For those who attempted to dismiss the thought of a threat as being an overstatement, let's not forget that China expanded its land mass by 50 percent when it invaded and occupied Tibet in the 1950s. Notice the disturbing pattern.

If China borders you or borders water that is anywhere near you, let's say the Pacific Ocean, it will assert every conceivable claim to wrest your sovereignty or territory from you, including threats, provocations, stunts, protests, and gunboat diplomacy, all while whining in the international forums that are available to it about its treatment, about how they're being treated. This is to say nothing of its routine conduct in international affairs: Industrial espionage; piracy; forced organ transplants by religious practitioners that it has murdered; IP violations; currency manipulation; and even bad and deadly dog food, I might add.

In the New York Times magazine's Sunday, October 27th, in an article entitled, "A Game of Shark and Minnow," the author writes,

> "China's currently in disputes with several of its neighbors. And the Chinese, having become decidedly more willing to wield a heavy stick, there is a growing sense that they have been waiting for a long time to flex their muscles. And that time has finally arrived."

Again, Farad Zakaria writes that, "Diplomats have worried that China has been circulating new maps of the region in which a previously dotted demarcation line that China claims in the South China Sea," instead of a dotted line, it now is a solid line. This is far from a new problem. Yet, the situation has not reserved the scrutiny that it does seriously deserve.

After a trip to the region, I reported to the House in late 1998, "The pattern of Chinese naval bases in the Spratly," meaning the Spratly Islands, "shows an encircling strategy of energy-rich islands and intimidating military presence along the vital sea route." I argued then "The U.S. Government must end its silence about the Chinese military buildup in the Spratly." Multiple administrations and Secretaries of State have, unfortunately, thought since then that we cannot disturb our second largest trading partner or that the situation they would hope will improve on its own.

Worse yet, the New York Times magazine piece reports, "The Americans pointedly refused to take sides in the sovereignty disputes.'' The magazine correctly notes, ''China's behavior as it becomes more powerful along with the freedom of navigation and control over the South China sea lanes, which are being threatened, will be among the major global political issues of the 21st Century.''

I would argue that to believe China's apparent expansionism is accidental or inevitable sells our adversary short. And we helped create this monster, this threat, by granting a permanent normal trade relations with what was then and still is the world's worse human rights abuser. This is something we never did with the Soviet Union. We never granted most favored nation status with the Soviet Union. And that is why Soviet communism went down and why dictatorship in China has emerged as a great threat to all of us, not just its own people.

There is a longstanding deliberate strategy in China to expand, provoke, challenge, and ultimately dominate the region and then the world. Stephanie Kleine-Ahlbrandt, the director of the Asia-Pacific programs at the United States Institute of Peace, said, ''Nothing in China happens overnight. Any move you see was planned and prepared for years, if not more. So, obviously, this maritime issue is very important to China.''

Our witnesses today paint a bleak and compelling picture. Steve Mosher has written prolifically on our topic today. Perry Pickert describes China playing a far more sophisticated game of statecraft than what we are playing. And Rick Fisher states succinctly, ''We are in a cold war with China.'' Far from minding its own business, as a good neighbor, China—and that is what they would do if they were minding their own business. China, instead, is an international menace with grand designs. Marxism may be on its last ash heap of a history, but Marxist-oriented one-party rule tragically has characterized China for more than 60 years.

Our Pentagon's announced strategy of a strategic pivot to Asia will be hollow if we are not clear about the main threat in this theater. Its maritime claims are dubious. Its grand designs must be opposed by the free world if peace is to be preserved.

[The prepared statement of Mr. Rohrabacher follows:]

4

SUBCOMMITTEE HEARING NOTICE
COMMITTEE ON FOREIGN AFFAIRS
U.S. HOUSE OF REPRESENTATIVES
WASHINGTON, D.C. 20515-6128
Subcommittee on Europe, Eurasia, and Emerging Threats
Dana Rohrabacher (R-CA), Chairman

China's Maritime and Other Geographic Threats

Good morning, the hearing is convened, I recognize myself for an opening statement.

Red China is *the threat* of the 21st Century. Since its birth as a Communist country 64 years ago this Friday, untold misery has fallen on the world's most populous nation. *Millions* killed in the Cultural Revolution of 50 years ago and regular repression since. Today, its extravagant claims do not allow for autonomy of belief or systems outside its control. It has staged a concerted effort against any religion that does not worship at the altar of Mao, be it any flavor of Buddhism, Christianity or other faiths. The Falun Gong and the Uyghurs have been singled out for special persecution.

To some, perhaps, Mao is a harmless print on a poster or a T-shirt. In reality, he joins the ranks of Hitler and Stalin as the 20th Century's worst, in butchering millions of his fellow citizens. One of our witnesses today, Steve Mosher, in his 2000 book *Hegemon: China's Plan to Dominate Asia and the World*, quotes Mao telling a "stunned" Khrushchev, "So what if we lose 300 million people. Our women will make it up in a generation." Lest one think Mao a dusty old historical anachronism, foreign policy columnist Fareed Zakaria writes in *The Washington Post*, October 24, "It appears that the party is choosing older, Mao-era methods of crackdowns, public confessions and purification campaigns."

What exactly does that mean? There are millions of prisoners of conscience today in labor camps. According to a new report by the Center for International Media Assistance for the National Endowment for Democracy, "China's media environment remained one of the world's most restrictive in 2012." "Crimes" as minor as "rumor mongering" on the Internet can land one in indefinite detention. Authorities censor and harass international reporters, or deny their visa applications or renewals. Physical attacks on foreign media members are a disturbing and growing trend.

And their long reach extends overseas. One of our witnesses today, Steve Mosher had his promising academic career in the United States as the first American social scientist allowed to carry out fieldwork in Mao's China derailed over outspoken criticism of China some years ago.

Today, we look at China's external posture toward its bordering states. It has menaced, threatened and even attempted to absorb its neighbors, most notably Tibet and Taiwan— and has clashes with virtually its every bordering state. The subcommittee will examine China's threatening maritime and territorial claims. For those tempted to dismiss the thought of a *threat* as an overstatement, let's not forget that China expanded its land mass by 50 percent when it invaded and occupied Tibet.

Notice the disturbing pattern: if China borders you or water anywhere near you (say, the Pacific Ocean), it will assert every conceivable claim to wrest your sovereignty or territory from you, including threats, provocations, stunts, protests and gunboat diplomacy, all the while whining in international forums about its treatment. This is to say nothing of its routine conduct in international affairs: industrial espionage, piracy, forced organ harvesting of religious practitioners, IP violations, currency manipulation, and even deadly dog food.

In *The New York Times Magazine* Sunday October 27, in an article entitled, "A Game of Shark and Minnow," the author writes "China is currently in disputes with several of its neighbors, and the Chinese having become decidedly more willing to wield a heavy stick. There is a growing sense that they have been waiting a long time to flex their muscles and that that time has finally arrived." Fareed Zakaria writes that, "Diplomats have worried that China has been circulating new maps of the region in which a previously dotted line demarcating Beijing's claims in the South China Sea now appears as a solid line."

This is far from a new problem, yet this situation has not reserved the scrutiny or seriousness it deserves. After a trip to the region, I reported to the House in late 1998, "The pattern of Chinese naval bases in the Spratlys shows an encircling strategy of the energy-rich islands and an intimidating military presence along the vital sea route." I argued then, "The U.S. Government must end its silence about the Chinese military buildup in the Spratlys." Multiple administrations and Secretaries of State have unfortunately thought we can't disturb our second largest trading partner or that the situation will improve on its own. Worse yet, *The New York Times Magazine* piece reports, "The Americans pointedly refuse to take sides in the sovereignty disputes."

The Magazine correctly notes, "China's behavior as it becomes more powerful, along with freedom of navigation and control over South China Sea shipping lanes, will be among the major global political issues of the 21st century." I would argue that to believe China's apparent expansionism is accidental or inevitable sells our adversaries short. And we helped create this monster by granting permanent normal trade relations (PNTR), something we never did for the Soviet Union.

There is a longstanding deliberate strategy to expand, provoke, challenge and ultimately dominate the region and then the world. Stephanie Kleine-Ahlbrandt, the director of Asia-Pacific programs at the United States Institute of Peace, said. "Nothing in China happens overnight. Any move you see was planned and prepared for years, if not more. So obviously this maritime issue is very important to China."

Our witnesses paint a bleak and compelling picture. Steve Mosher has written prolifically on our topic today, Perry Pickert describes a China playing a far more sophisticated game of statecraft than we are, and Rick Fisher states it succinctly, "We Are in a Cold War with China."

Far from minding its own business as a good neighbor, China is an international menace with grand designs. Marxism may be on the ash heap of history, but Marxist oriented one-party rule tragically has characterized China for more than 60 years. Our Pentagon's announced strategy of a strategic pivot to Asia will be hollow if we are not clear about the main threat in the theater. Its maritime claims are dubious; its grand designs must be opposed by the free world.

———————

Mr. ROHRABACHER. And, with that, I would ask my ranking member for his opening statement.

Mr. KEATING. Well, thank you, Mr. Chairman, for holding this hearing. I would like to thank you and thank all of our witnesses for appearing today.

I will make note that one of the witnesses is Dr. Peter Sandby-Thomas, a visiting professor from University of Massachusetts in my own district. And I appreciate your being here today, as I appreciate all of the witnesses for being here today and look forward to your testimony.

We are joined by Representative Lowenthal. Welcome.

The United States has a clear national interest in promoting the peaceful resolution of maritime and other territorial disputes in Asia. Since World War II, the United States has played the leading role in maintaining peace and stability in the Pacific. It is, therefore, appropriate that the United States have an active and direct role in resolving the disputes in the South and East China Seas. Yet, we must be sure that our policies and actions do not inadvertently heighten regional tensions.

China's maritime and territorial disputes with its neighbors date back to conflicts of the Nineteenth and 20th Centuries. Most were seriously exacerbated by the tensions of the Cold War. In addition, most of these disputes have deep historical roots and are fought with bitter emotion. Achieving their peaceful resolution will not be easy. It is, therefore, essential that the United States continue to support a collaborative process free of aggression, coercion, or the threat of force amongst all parties involved. This will require patience, perseverance, and deft diplomacy on our part, even as tensions in the region continue to escalate.

The United States has made clear it will uphold our security commitments and treaty allies and partners in the region. And we will make sure that we are strong in stating that. Now is not the right time to change that tact. In that regard, continued U.S. support for the development of a multilateral code of conduct between China and the association in southeast Asian nations is essential. A binding code of conduct would considerably reduce tensions in this region.

I applaud the administration's effort to ensure freedom of the navigational rights in this region as well as new initiatives to help allies and partners strengthen their capacity to patrol and administer their territorial waters. I am, however, concerned over the impact that across-the-board budget cuts and related uncertainty will have on these important programs and U.S. projection in the region. I look forward to hearing our panelists' views on the immediacy of the threat posed by maritime disputes and the effectiveness of the U.S. policies in the region along with your own thoughts on how the United States might more effectively press claimants to peacefully resolve their differences.

With that, I yield back, Mr. Chairman.

Mr. ROHRABACHER. We are joined by Mr. Lowenthal, but, Mr. Stockman, do you have an opening statement?

Mr. STOCKMAN. Just briefly. To our detriment, in the 1940s, we ignored Asia and didn't pay attention to it. And I think that was obvious when Pearl Harbor happened. Well, theoretically it caught us by surprise. And now again we seem to be putting the Asia problems on the back burner.

When we visited with the Prime Minister from Japan, he expressed concern that America is losing its interest in Asia and its will to defend Asia and our allies, such as Japan. I also remember in 2008, the Olympics. One young man got up and screamed out,—this was in Tiananmen Square—"We are a nation of slaves. Where is America?" And he was hauled off.

And the reporter glibly said, "Well, we don't know whatever happened to that young man." I think it is high time that we take more of a look at what is going on in Asia and be more sensitive and be more alert. I think down the road, by not following that path, we are going to end up in big trouble. And it will be very much like 9/11, where we wonder what happened, where were we. It will catch us off guard. Why didn't we connect the dots? Well, the dots are all there. We need to connect them.

And I appreciate these gentlemen coming forward today and actually connecting the dots. And this is going to be part of the record that we are going to have. So when we look back on it, we can look at this record. And a lot of you will probably say, "We told you so." So I appreciate you coming out today and giving your testimony. And I yield back the balance.

Mr. PICKERT. No. I am just pleased to be here.

Mr. LOWENTHAL. I am pleased he is here, too.

Mr. ROHRABACHER. All right. Thank you, Mr. Lowenthal.

Our witnesses, we have some very significant witnesses today. And what I am going to do is ask, with permission of the panel, that we place their very lengthy backgrounds and their credentials into the record. And so if we could just put their bios in the record? I am just going to announce them. And then we will proceed. And I would ask that you would be giving us about 5 minutes and then the rest of your testimony for the record. And then we will have some questions and answers.

So first we have Mr. Perry Pickert. He is a Ph.D. and a retired intelligence officer and I guess a very continuing intelligent person. So, Doctor, would you please proceed? And then we will introduce the other witnesses. And your lengthy bio will be made a part of the record.

Mr. PICKERT. Thank you very much for inviting me.

STATEMENT OF PERRY PICKERT, PH.D., RETIRED CAREER INTELLIGENCE OFFICER

Mr. PICKERT. But I wonder how we can wake up my PowerPoint, which has been put to sleep. I will start. They should be able to push a button and turn on the computer, but I don't know what happened.

Mr. ROHRABACHER. Has someone hacked into our system?

Mr. PICKERT. Yes. The Chinese are here already and shutting me out. But I will begin anyway without the PowerPoint. I can run through it fairly quickly.

Mr. ROHRABACHER. It has showing up on a television set.

Mr. PICKERT. The term "Great Game" was coined in the early 18th Century to describe the strategy and tactics to protect India, the jewel of the crown of the British Empire, from a rising Russia.

Beginning with Woodrow Wilson's Fourteen Points, the United States has advocated substituting universal international organizations and the rule of law for the great power competition and war.

President Obama at the U.N. General Assembly this fall, stepping into the stage of one of the Great Games of this century, said, "There is no Great Game to be won."

In this century, the United Nations system provides the normative and institutional structure for relations as well as the language of diplomacy. While Russia, China, and the United States have never fought a war against each other, the United Nations have provided the legal rationale and cover for actions of their military and clandestine services.

This morning, I will survey the strategic landscape in Asia focused on a rising China's territorial claims and the implications for the United States. China and Russia view the world from a long-term perspective of the Russians as a chessboard, and the Chinese play Go.

Mr. ROHRABACHER. There you got it [referring to PowerPoint presentation].

Mr. PICKERT. I got it up but not connected to this yet. There we go. Now we have got it. Now it should work.

I will use the traditional Chinese game of Go, which is played by placing stones on a board, black and white stones. They are not like chess pieces, which can go anywhere, but they essentially capture territory. Territory in this game is really the space between points, and the Go pieces are placed on the intersection of the squares.

Traditional China is at the center of its own universe and over the centuries has grown from a very small tribe in central China to the outside. Its international relations were handled as family relations. And the outlying princes were ruled as if in a family, with the closer relatives closer and the further relatives further away. But on the outside, we're the barbarians who were ruled liked dogs, being rewarded and punished with bones, rewards; and sticks. The Ming dynasty extended throughout the whole of East Asia and established a system of tribute whereby the rituals of kowtowing and coming to the center with presents. Today the center is a U.N. General Assembly in New York, every year from October until December.

Now, if you look at this map, we will go to look at the Senkaku Islands, which are the first territorial dispute. You will notice they can hardly be seen on this map. That exaggerates their size drastically. This is what the Senkakus look like in the picture. There are three small little islands.

In Go terms, this would be played as a three-sided game of Go with a space. This game is almost completely finished. The contesting space out there now is the blank spaces between the lines. And those are called points. So that there is no real territory as ground. It is territorial space.

This is what Taiwan looks at from this perspective. You can hardly find Quemoy and Matsu on a map, but you can see Taiwan off of the islands, a distance of the straits away. As a Go problem, this is the Goggle map of Quemoy and Matsu. It is on Google because it is Taiwanese territory and, therefore, is open to the word—

but it is, you will see, completely surrounded on three sides, leaving only one open. In Go terms, this is called atari. When you bring someone into position where they are about to be surrounded, you are supposed to inform your opponent that they are in atari. Generally it is not necessary to put another stone there because you don't need to finish that off. You have got that territory able to be captured by one stone.

These are fuel air explosives shot from artillery rounds in Syria today. The reason I say, "Welcome to Grozny" is that with this method, after Putin got tired of having an inconclusive battle in Chechnya, he used fuel air explosives to essentially level the town in 2000. Fuel air explosives are like napalm, which is blown by artillery shells. It spreads out and then is ignited after the cloud is lighted. That not only makes a big explosion, but it also sucks out the oxygen from the area. And, of course, they could use fewer explosives to blow Quemoy off the face of the Earth in 2 seconds.

These are China's maritime claims in the South China Sea. In this case, the empty spaces usually are the specks out in the middle of the lake, which are the essentially disputed islands. The far red line shows where the disputes are. Viewed it as a Go game, you will see that these are the six parties about to contest over a little spot in there. The Chinese way of handling this will be to do it bilaterally, waiting for weakness on the part of one side, then taking the space.

This is the Chinese latest surface-to-sir intermediate-range ballistic missile. It has a fuel air explosive warhead and is called the aircraft carrier killer because, in fact, if it hit right on the aircraft carrier, it would be able to kill everyone on it and surround, and that would be the end of it. Of course, it is really just a big SCUD. And the Russians and the Chinese do not use single missile tactics. They use mass tactics. So they would fire eight to ten of these. This is the range of the missile, the intermediate ones. And that shows the range of all of the other. In the game of Go, this would essentially put the entire area that we were talking about under the range of non-nuclear ballistic missiles that can be fired. And they are mobile. So we have no clue where they are. And a response is preempted by the longer range potential of nuclear missiles which as you can see can hit the United States easily.

This is the Tibetan Plateau. And you can see on this map that the center, the one little corner, of Tibet is the source of all of the rivers of Southwest Asia: India, China, Vietnam, Burma. The Chinese tactic with respect to this is to dam part of these rivers up in China. So at any time, they can simply turn off the water for Southeast Asia or let it out, causing floods. They have a series of dams in China. And there are quite a few dams that are built in cooperation with the other countries, which they are sponsoring.

The India-China border is the furthest west. This is an area where the Go strategy is to "seize the high ground." It's not really necessary for them to have forces on the area and if they were at Aksai Chin, they would be up at about 14,000 feet needing oxygen equipment. So nobody ever actually sits up there, but they have skirmishes all of the time.

Now we will turn to the U.N. system as a place for the competition of the Chinese world view. First you can see that the Russians also have a view of the U.N. That is the U.N. flag with a hammer and a sickle and the territory that they used to think they controlled. This is the way the Chinese view the U.N. system as they expand their influence over it.

Now I will go through the specific organs of the U.N., but I am going to drop the Go analogy because it is a little complicated. The General Assembly is what I would call ''liars' poker.'' If you look on there, you will see Khrushchev with his boot on the table. He, of course, actually had two very fine Italian shoes on at the time and brought that along only as a prop. He didn't take off his shoe and pound it on the table. And Deng Xiaoping announced his strategy for the next 20 years. I will be through in 2 seconds here.

The Security Council is strip poker. You go in, think one thing. And by the time that the Russians and Chinese get finished with the resolution, you get another.

The Shanghai Cooperative Organization was created by the Chinese and the Russians for central Asia. You can see its logo is essentially the trace of Mongol Empire. I call this the KGB officers' and agents' traveling crap game.

The Law of the Sea Convention has been signed by China and Russia. And the U.S. is not a member. So we don't participate. This will show you how the U.N. system allows you to stretch to the Pacific where you can see the Law of the Sea pioneer investors, the Chinese, the Russians, and the French, having staked out territory at the bottom of the ocean. The competing claim is the Clipperton Island claim, which the U.S. has based on the economic zone.

Finally, my conclusion is how do you capture Kim's gun, which is in Lahore, Pakistan? And the answer is to recruit the Lama—as you see, he was sitting there—because you control the space by having the person who was controlling the person on the space.

And this was Kipling's statement about the Great Game, the final bottom line, ''When everyone is dead, the Great Game is finished,'' not as we have seen the American view that it has been subsumed into the U.N. system.

Thank you.

[The prepared statement of Mr. Pickert follows:]

The Great Game in 21st Century Asia

Perry L. Pickert

"There's no Great Game to be won."

- President Obama at the UN General Assembly

The term "Great Game" was coined in the early 1800's to describe the strategy and tactics to protect India, the jewel in the crown of the British Empire, from a rising Russia. Beginning with Woodrow Wilson's Fourteen Points the United States has advocated substituting a universal international organization based on the rule of law for the great power competition and war.

In the 21st Century, the United Nations system provides the normative and institutional structure for international relations as well as the language of diplomacy. While Russia, China and the United States have never fought a declared war, the League of Nations and the United Nations have provided legal rationale and cover for the actions of their military forces and clandestine services.

This morning, I will survey the strategic landscape of Asia focused on a rising China's territorial and maritime disputes and consider the implications for the United States. China and Russia view the world from the long-term perspective of participants in the Great Game. The Chinese play go and the Russians chess, while at UN this fall President Obama asserted United States was not engaged in a "zero-sum endeavor."

For a next few minutes, I will try to get within Chinese strategic thinking by sketching the territorial disputes on China's periphery as if they were to be played on a go board. I will consider the traditional mix of hard and soft power as it has been used over the centuries as the Chinese played the Great Game first in Central Asia and now across the world within the UN system.

China at the Center

The word for China means central kingdom. The state began as warring feudal lords finally dominated by the most powerful among them. Endless conflict eventually lead to the dominant kingdom unifying the country and establishing a highly centralized government based on a model of hierarchical family relations with the emperor at the top. He was considered the ruler of "all under heaven" which meant the world as civilized by Chinese culture. Those outside were considered barbarians and were managed by bones (rewards) and sticks (punishments). Written history in China generally is traced to the Shang Dynasty which tells of China's First Emperor Ch'in Shih Huang (259 BC – 210 BC). International relations evolved through Zhou, Qin, Han, Sui, Tang, Song, Yuan, Ming, and Qing dynasties with a highly ritualized system of diplomacy and trade described as tribute to the Emperor.

The Game of go as Strategic Model

The source of power in ancient China was agricultural land so go is played on a plane grid of 19 horizontal and 19 vertical lines called a board. The players are given as many black or white stones as necessary. Unlike chess or checkers the opposing stones are not killed or counted. Instead stones are captured by completely surrounding the opposing players stones. It generally takes five or six moves to surround even empty territory, and many more to capture an opposing player's stone. All moves take place in plain sight so strategy and deception are keys to victory.

Asia as a Go Board

In order to consider China's territorial disputes as a strategic game it is merely necessary to imagine a map of China with a grid of horizontal and vertical lines. Chinese military forces and those of the bordering countries will be for the sake of the game deployed as they are actually positioned today. For the sake of my discussion, the rapprochement between Russia and China in the early 1990's settled the various territorial claims. It was followed by withdrawal of significant military forces by both sides. To begin with the go board will be focused on the Asian continent and the surrounding waters:

1. The China – India Border Disputes – Seize the high ground
2. Tibet – Send Han, recruit the monks
3. The Mekong River- Grab them by the throat
4. The South China Sea – Divide and Conquer
5. Senkaku/Diaoyu Islands – Just a Point
6. Kinmen (Quemoy) - Atari
7. Taiwan – East Wind

From the strategic perspective of space and population as reflected in go, the bottom line is that none of the peripheral territorial disputes are critical to China's economy or territorial integrity. The territory on the Himalayan ridgeline between India and China is the only territory of strategic significance. It is important as a back door to China and need not be occupied by China, only denied to another great power. i.e. India. Tibet is another question. The Chinese have gone beyond treating its autonomous zone as a border and are gradually filling in the space with Han Chinese.

The game of go is between two players. China's traditional imperial diplomacy with China at the center would treat each of the separate peripheral spaces bilaterally so that the opponent would have to deal one-one where China has a huge relative advantage. In the 21st Century China is one of 190 or so sovereign states presumed to have legal equality. Yet each has a unique territorial space on the globe with a unique configuration of relations with every other state.

Global Go

China's participation in the current system of international relations may also be viewed as projection of the Great Game strategy on to a go board to the UN system. Over Churchill's objections, President Roosevelt insisted the Chinese be included in the wartime alliance and as permanent members of the UN Security Council. The PRC took the UN seat from Taiwan in 1971 and now pursues China's traditional Great Game objectives within the legal and institutional framework of the UN system.

- Permanent Membership on the UN Security Council granted automatic great power status and veto over any UN binding resolution or anti-Chinese coercive action
- Shanghai Cooperative Organization (SCO) was created with the Russians and some former Soviet satellites in 2001- it is a regional organization within the UN system the to counterbalance the EU and NATO
- UN General Assembly and other deliberative and distributive UN organs - China has joined Russian and the non-aligned caucus to form their own Like-Minded Group to press their programs and protect their interests
- Participation in the UN Law of the Sea Treaty gives China political advantage in UN forums

Each of the UN organizations has different functions and political cultures so it is necessary to consider China's territorial disputes within each organization:

(1) China – India Boarder Disputes – China's veto offers protection but UK and US generally support India
(2) Tibet –Taiwan and the PRC had virtually identical positions on Tibet so PRC inherited positions protected in both the Security Council and the General Assembly but today faces competitive votes on human rights
(3) The Mekong River Commission makes decisions by consensus but China is building upstream dams on territory it controls
(4) The South China Sea – China has recently refused to participate in arbitration required by the Law of the Sea Treaty as requested by the Philippines
(5) Senkaku/Diaoyu Islands – A trilateral dispute with Japan opposed to both the PRC and Taiwan
(6) Kinmen (Quemoy) – Peaceful at the moment
(7) Taiwan – the UN battle was lost when the PRC took the China seat

For twenty years the PRC kept a low profile posture in the UN. It used its veto sparingly only when direct interests were threatened such as over Taiwan. Recently, China has developed a comprehensive global presence in the UN system and has developed a web of alliances to block adverse political actions of any kind. With respect to territorial issues it has the veto power and political backing to ignore the UN and deal with countries on a bilateral basis.

Mr. ROHRABACHER. We are going to now go to the last witness because he happens to be the witness who was invited by the ranking member, and I would like Ranking Member Gideon to introduce his witness today.

Mr. KEATING. Thank you, Mr. Chairman.

I won't go into great detail because time is precious today, but I do thank Dr. Sandby-Thomas for joining us today and to testify on these issues. I do think his own expertise will be self-evident. And, rather than delay with an introduction, I will just introduce Dr. Sandby-Thomas. Thank you.

STATEMENT OF PETER SANDBY–THOMAS, PH.D., VISITING LECTURER OF POLITICAL SCIENCE, UNIVERSITY OF MASSA-CHUSETTS DARTMOUTH

Mr. SANDBY-THOMAS. All right. Thank you.

Chairman Rohrabacher, Ranking Member Keating, members of the committee, thank you for the opportunity to testify before the Subcommittee on Europe, Eurasia, and Emerging Threats on this topic of vital national and geopolitical significance.

Sort of to frame the discussion, I think it is important to consider the question of whether China's recent behavior, both maritime and beyond, should be construed as a threat. In sort of making that point, the purpose is to draw attention to the fact that China is emerging as a reasonable and possibly global power. And so in such a context, it is necessary to determine what types of behavior and conduct are justifiable and commensurate with this increasing power when you clarify this and do not provide the benefit in terms of assessing China's behavior in terms of what's threatening and what is, say, permissible.

If we turn to China's military capabilities, it is clear that they have expanded rapidly in recent years. And that is aided in large part through a concerted effort to allocate increasing budget spending toward their military. And if we looked sort of within this, you can see that the People's Liberation Army has navy capabilities. They have been notably expanded. You have seen sort of significant milestones in terms of China's first aircraft carrier, plans for a second one, sort of details indicating that they have other sort of high-tech equipment, sort of guided missile destroyers, et cetera, et cetera. One of the aspects of this is that it is not always entirely clear how to determine the veracity of such reports, which in and of itself can be perceived as an issue in terms of transparency. And sometimes that leaves a void that gets filled by increased speculation.

But, regardless of that, I think it seems clear that the navy is rapidly developing and is on course to be the dominant maritime power in east Asia. The time frame is not exactly clear, but it seems within the next 10 to 20 years. There doesn't appear to be another rival that is capable of sort of challenging it. The only sort of reasonable one would be Japan, but it is obviously sort of hobbled by constitutional restrictions.

At this point, I think, though, the focus is often sort of solely on the hardware. And that is, of course, important, but it is also important to consider sort of how seaworthy China's vessels are. That is not exactly clear. These things aren't obviously battle-tested.

They also have a limited schedule of sea operations. And I think another aspect to consider is, say, the sort of quality of the mariners that China has. Again, that is something that can be put down to a lack of practice, certainly when you compare it to, say, the U.S. naval capabilities.

Nevertheless, the expansion of naval capabilities has raised concerns, particularly over China's intentions. And this has led to, you know, a different—I was drawing different conclusions. Some make the point that this expansion definitively reflects an intention to exert regional dominance. And I think that this—it is not obviously something that can necessarily be ruled out.

Certainly, you know, why does China invest all of this money and certainly equipment if it doesn't intend to use it? That is certainly the prevailing logic. But I think the more lightly explanation is that China's strategy, certainly in the near to medium term, is primarily defensive in nature, rather than offensive.

If we look at the region that it is located in, it is corrupted by, say, a number of conflicting and competing challenges. It is a region that is filled with historical grievances. You have competing powers, such as Australia also has a naval fleet. And Japan has impressive capabilities, even if, to a degree, limited. You also have, say, unpredictable actors that are in the region. And so the conclusion that I would draw is that China's naval expansion would appear to be more geared toward ensuring their own territorial security as well as ensuring that sea lanes of communication remain open for commercial interests.

And while this assessment does run counter to prevailing orthodoxy and it is clear that in the past few years, a label of "assertive" has been attached to China, particularly with regards to the East China and South China Seas and while the nature of this claim I think is, say, ambiguous, sort of elastic, if you will, isn't clearly grounded, I think you can look that China's behavior in these situations has not significantly deviated from past practices. You can argue that there has been provocation on the part of others. So other actors need to be taken into account.

And I think you can make the point that, you know, China has been, say, more forthright in pressing its own claims, but whether—I don't think that you can argue in both cases that the claims are significantly new. Generally China uses a designation of core national interest to determine if it regards a particular territory as non-negotiable. And that has not been the case on both the Senkaku/Diaoyu Island dispute or the dispute in the South China Seas.

So, because of time, I will sort of wrap up and just say in terms of implications for the U.S. in these regional developments, the particular concern seems to be, say, a security point of view. I think that you can make sort of arguments about sort of the assertiveness of China's behavior, but, regardless of that, I think the dispute between China and Japan appears to be the more serious. I don't think that the intention is to engage in conflict, but it is clear that there are increased Chinese incursions, increased Japanese responses. And so that increases the likelihood or the potentiality for some sort of conflict. And obviously that, then, brings in the U.S. and its security obligations. In terms of the South China Sea, it seems that negotiated compromise is more likely and possible and something that the U.S. should certainly press for.

[The prepared statement of Mr. Sandby-Thomas follows:]

House Committee on Foreign Affairs

Subcommittee on Europe, Eurasia, and Emerging Threats

Hearing on "China's Maritime and Other Threats"

October 30, 2013

Written Statement

By

Peter Sandby-Thomas, PhD

Visiting Professor in Political Science

University of Massachusetts Dartmouth

Chairman Rohrabacher, Ranking Member Keating, members of the Committee: Thank you for the opportunity to testify before the Subcommittee on Europe, Eurasia, and Emerging Threats on a topic of such national and geopolitical significance.

Turning to this topic, I would like to begin by considering the question of whether China's recent behavior, maritime and beyond, should be construed as a "threat". In so doing, the purpose is to draw attention to the obvious fact that China is an emerging regional and, possibly, global power and, in such a context, to determine what types of behavior and conduct are justifiable and commensurate with this increasing power. The need for clarification on this point will be of benefit in assessing the threats, if any, posed by China.

China's military capabilities have clearly expanded in recent years, aided in large part through year-on-year double-digit increases in budget allocations. Within this, investment in the upgrading of the People's Liberation Army Navy's (PLAN) capabilities has been notable, with the launch of China's first aircraft carrier viewed as a significant step forward. Moreover, speculation suggests that a second carrier is already underway along with the approval of designs for guided-missile destroyers (DDGs). Leaving aside the veracity of such reports, the prevailing view is that the PLAN is rapidly developing and is on course to be the dominant maritime power in the East Asia in the next 10-20 years. A couple of points can be interjected at this point, namely the full extent and seaworthiness of China's vessels are difficult to accurately gauge, both due to a limited schedule of sea operations as well as a lack of engagement i.e. conflict. An additional consideration–hardware is an important aspect of naval expansion but not the only one–an extremely important part. Nevertheless, the significant investment in the expansion of naval capabilities has raised concerns over China's intentions. For some, the conclusion to be drawn is that this expansion reflects an intention to exert regional dominance in the East Asia region. And while such a conclusion cannot be ruled out, it appears that the more likely explanation is that China's strategy in the near- to medium-term at least is primarily defensive in nature than offensive. The region in which China is located features historical grievances (e.g. Vietnam, Japan), competing (naval) powers (e.g. Taiwan, Australia, Japan) as well as unpredictable actors (e.g. North Korea). As such, China's naval expansion would appear to be more geared towards ensuring its own territorial security as well as ensuring Sea Lanes of Communication remain open for commercial interests, including trade and energy.

The above assessment does run counter to the prevailing orthodoxy concerning China in the past few years, in which it has repeatedly been labeled as "assertive". This has been particularly the case in its pressing of territorial claims in both the East China and South China Seas. Leaving aside the inherent ambiguity of such a label, it is possible to argue in both situations that China's behavior did not significantly deviate from past practices and that the role of other actors in these situations must be taken into account. In the case of the East China Sea and the dispute with Japan over the Senkaku/Diaoyu Islands, the decision by Japan to accede to the purchase of three of the islands from a private Japanese citizen was the most recent catalyst for action and reaction. Indeed, though the Japanese government's action did not, in practice, change anything i.e. Japan still administers the Islands and its territorial waters, it did, from the Chinese point of view, undermine the status quo. And while the Chinese response has taken the form of repeated incursions into Japanese waters, it has not determined the islands to be a "core national interest" while leaving open the possibility of negotiating the status of the Islands. That said, it seems clear that part of the strategy engaged in by Beijing is to successively undermine the legitimacy of Japan's claims over the Islands. The Islands themselves hold little intrinsic value, their ownership is being contested because of the location of energy reserves in the seabed adjacent to the islands and, from China's point of view, offering a strategic access point through the "first Island Chain" that would enable it to reach the Western Pacific Ocean. On the first point, negotiations have taken place on the possible joint exploration of the energy resources; however, on the second point, it is unclear what form a resolution will take, particularly given the current state of political relations between China and Japan. As for the South China Sea, the dispute in this region was prompted in part by the deadlines imposed by UN Convention on the Law of the Sea (UNCLOS). In its submissions, China's claims to the entire South China Sea region are not entirely new and not as comprehensive as commonly thought. Moreover, in response to the actions of other states, notably Vietnam and the Philippines, China maritime agencies has increased patrols of this area and engaged in acts including detention of fishing boats and the cutting of cables in survey boats. China's interest in this region appears to be both security- and commercially-related. Indeed, given that the South China Sea is a major shipping route for many countries, including the US, it is an area of strategic significance. Considering the possibility of resolution, China's recent actions notwithstanding, it remains involved in the process to build on the Declaration on the Conduct of Parties in the South China Sea (DOC) that was signed between ASEAN and China in 2002.

As for the implications for the US in these regional developments, the area of particular concern from a security point of view is with the dispute between China and Japan in the East China Sea. The reasoning for this is twofold: firstly, the US has affirmed its commitment to defend Japan following the passage of the 2013 U.S. National Defense Authorization Act; and secondly, this leaves US security, to some extent, being determined by other actors, in this case China and Japan. As the comments by Prime Minister Abe in the Wall Street Journal over the weekend, this situation is still inflamed. Moreover, with increased incursions by China and Japanese responses, the likelihood for clashes, accidental or otherwise, is increased.

Mr. ROHRABACHER. Well, thank you very much. And we will have questions for the panel as we finish our testimony. Next we have Rick Fisher, who is a senior fellow, Asian Military Affairs at the International Assessment and Strategy Center, as well as a lengthy bio as well, which will be submitted for the record.

Mr. Fisher, you may proceed with your testimony.

STATEMENT OF MR. RICK FISHER, SENIOR FELLOW, ASIAN MILITARY AFFAIRS, INTERNATIONAL ASSESSMENT AND STRATEGY CENTER

Mr. FISHER. Chairman Rohrabacher, Ranking Member Keating, and distinguished members of this subcommittee, I would also like to thank you for this privilege to offer testimony to aid your deliberations. I would also like to offer my compliment to your leadership in looking beyond Europe and Eurasia to examine concerns with China.

Just 2 weeks ago, I was called to address a NATO parliamentary committee on Chinese military modernization. And my experience at this meeting was that, indeed, there is great concern, especially when considering how China is pursuing its territorial claims in a way that is increasing the chances for conflict, either accidental or by design. I will just offer that just this past weekend, the Japanese Air Force had to scramble three times 3 days in a row to intercept threatening Chinese bombers that were conducting coordinated ship, submarine, and aircraft anti-ship exercises south of the Sakashima Islands, which if the Chinese ever succeed in grabbing the Senkaku Islands will be the next meal on the menu.

In my testimony, I try to describe how China is building a force to achieve regional dominance. I estimate that absent a countervailing effort by the United States and its allies, that China could have its regional dominance by early in the next decade. This dominance is going to be expressed not just in hardware, expansive space control, missiles, expanded regional nuclear forces, fourth and fifth generation aircraft, naval forces with multiple aircraft carriers, a large amphibious projection capability, but China will practice and will have the skills to use this hardware to achieve its aims.

Japan, of course, as I mentioned, is the target of the moment. Since the Japanese Government moved to purchase the Senkaku Islands in the Summer of 2012, a move which we have just found out was designed to try to ameliorate conflict with Beijing, the Chinese have put on an expanded paramilitary campaign to try to intimidate Japan into making concessions. It is not going to work. And my prediction is that the Japanese are going to rearm significantly because of this pressure and we will have a much more dangerous and more well-armed East China Sea by the end of this decade.

But China probably believes that it can have more success in the South China Sea. It is succeeding in the last year in pushing the Philippines away from areas near its economic exclusion zone. Mr. Chairman, as you pointed out, in a recent New York Times article, Chinese Coast Guard ships are trying to dissuade the Philippines from supplying men on a beached LST on the Second Thomas Shoal.

In the future, China is going to be building the means for global power projection. And it is going to be able to weigh in on other people's, other countries' territorial disputes. I would just offer that this year, I was able to find out by visiting arm shows that Argentina and China are considering the co-production of a Chinese fighter, a fighter that could be armed with a new Chinese hypersonic missile at a speed at which you can't shoot it down. China fully supports Argentina's claim to the Falklands. By the next decade, by the end of the next decade, will China be able to send aircraft carriers or amphibious groups to respond to a British attempt to defend the Falklands again?

I conclude by noting that while the Obama administration's recent pivot to Asia over the last 2 to 3 years has been welcomed in the region, the momentum that the administration has built up is being undermined significantly by uncertainty surrounding our ability to pay for new programs to make good on our pledges and continue to ensure pledges that we have made to our allies, our military allies. We are not able to afford aerial exercises that we have planned. We are threatening to cut back our number of carrier battle groups and eliminate whole types of combat aircraft. This is very disturbing. And it will only encourage the Chinese to press harder.

I believe we can deter China. I think we have it within our capability to encourage our allies to join a regional information-sharing network: Radar, space assets and the such, and then eventually tie this network to new ballistic missile capabilities: Short-range and medium-range systems that perhaps we share with our allies, intermediate-range systems that we deploy ourselves. If we can prove to China that, like on Dr. Pickert's Go board, that if they use their Navy, they can lose their Navy, then we can sustain deterrence and suggest to our Chinese friends that violence will not pay.

Thank you very much.

[The prepared statement of Mr. Fisher follows:]

China's Maritime and Other Geographic Threats

**Testimony by Richard D. Fisher, Jr., Senior Fellow,
International Assessment and Strategy Center**

**Before The Subcommittee on Europe, Eurasia and Emerging Threats,
Foreign Affairs Committee of the United States House of Representatives,
October 30, 2013**

Mr. Chairman and Distinguished Members of this Subcommittee:

The People's Republic of China has active and/or dormant territorial disputes with practically all of its neighbors. China is today using paramilitary or military force to assert its territorial or economic zone claims against Japan, Taiwan, the Philippines, Vietnam and India. China also continues its more than two-decade long preparations for war against democratic Taiwan. Despite a relative peace that exists between them today, there is sufficient indication that China could in the future opt to pursue latent territorial claims against Russia, Mongolia and Korea. China's key goal in the pursuit of its claims is to improve its geostrategic position in order to strengthen the dictatorship of the ruling Chinese Communist Party (CCP). But as the Party's insecurity increases, it cannot be determined how much it will "externalize" its internal contradictions by pursuing aggression, which then further justifies internal repression.

Fundamental to the CCP's pursuit of its territorial goals has been the buildup and increasingly assertive employment of the People's Liberation Army (PLA) and associated paramilitary forces, especially the newly reformed Chinese Coast Guard. China's use of military pressure in pursuit of its territorial claims is increasing the prospect for military clashes, especially with Japan and the Philippines. This testimony will largely focus on two concerns: 1) how China is building up and using its military forces to pursue its regional goals; and 2) how China is now building the framework for global military projection capabilities.

While China and the United States do not have direct territorial or resource disputes, Beijing's military buildup and intimidation of U.S. allies is intended to challenge Washington's ability to defend its allies, and thereby diminish the credibility of U.S. alliance commitments in East Asia. For most of the last year Japan has been in a near constant state of non-violent engagement with China's military and paramilitary forces over control of the Senkaku/Daiyou Islands, but the chances of a military incident are increasing. The Philippines is also being pushed by Chinese forces from areas in or near its Economic Exclusion Zone (EEZ). While the U.S. has become more critical of China's aggressiveness, it maintains a strict neutrality toward conflicting maritime territorial claims in East Asia. This neutrality was more convenient when the U.S. had an excess of military superiority, which is now eroding as China builds up its military. The Obama Administration's "Rebalance" or "Pivot" of 2011 to 2013 has been welcome. However, the impact of sequestration and other budget cuts and pressures have damaged the credibility of Washington's ability to prevail in the ongoing arms race with China.

When Will China Be Satisfied ?

When examining the number of China's territorial conflicts with its neighbors, and especially the degree to which it willing to undertake aggression against both powerful and weak neighbors, it is necessary to ask: at what point will the leadership of China be satisfied? China does not specify what level of control it desires over the South China Sea, the East China Sea or Taiwan. While "unification" or the conquest of Taiwan has long been called a "core interest," or an interest which China is willing to fight for, the term "core interest" has in recent years also been loosely applied to the South and East China Sea. China also has a policy of domestically cultivating resentment and of reaching back into history, when previous Chinese Emperors allegedly controlled areas far beyond present-day China, to justify current claims.

One ominous indicator from the deep well of nationalist sentiments in China is a list that has been posted and refined on Chinese web pages since at least 2008, called, "The Six Wars To Be Fought By China In the Coming 50 Years." Most recently it was posted in July 2013 on the web forum of the pro-Beijing and prominent Hong Kong newspaper *Wen Wei Po*. It includes:

1. The Unification of Taiwan (2020 to 2025)
2. "Reconquest" of the Spratly Islands (2035 to 2030)
3. "Reconquest" of Southern Tibet (2035 to 2040). Further goal of dismembering India.
4. "Reconquest" of Daiyou and Ryukyu Islands (2040 to 2045)
5. Unification of Outer Mongolia (2045 to 2050)
6. Taking back of lands lost to Russia (2055 to 2060)

This "Six Wars" list itself cannot be linked to any formal Chinese government policy or strategy. It is also somewhat assuring that on Chinese web pages, as many Chinese readers seem to condemn this list with horror as seem to support it. It may be tempting to dismiss this list as nationalist ranting. But it is also a fact that by means short of war, China is now trying to accomplish the first two, while the second two are being pursued partially.

Until July 2012 it could easily have been considered an extreme assessment to state that China would want to "reconquer" the Ryukyu Islands -- which China abandoned its claims to as part of the Treaty of Shimonoseki in 1895, after its defeat in the First Sino-Japanese War. In July 2012 PLA General Luo Yuan, known for voicing hard-line nationalist opinions, questioned Japan's sovereignty over the Ryukyus, and repeated this opinion to Chinese journalists in May 2013. Then on 9 May 2013 a Chinese Foreign Ministry spokesman rejected Japanese protests that China's state-controlled media would challenge Japan's sovereignty over the Ryukyus, but did not disavow that challenge. While it may not be possible today to determine the extent of China's future territorial ambitions, it is possible to assess the kind of military they are developing that could employed to that end, how it is using its forces today to pursue territorial goals, how its neighbors are reacting, and what risks China's actions pose for the U.S..

Building Forces For Regional Dominance

Soon after the June 1989 Tiananmen Massacre, the Chinese Communist Party leadership quietly abandoned former paramount leader Deng Xiaoping's 1980s policy of putting military modernization at a 4th level of national priority and very likely raised to a top level of priority. The stellar U.S. performance during the 1990-1991 Gulf War against Iraq further confirmed this CCP decision. Today, after 20 years of sustained effort, it can be said that the People's Liberation Army has largely accomplished a transition to a 4th Generation level of technology and is quickly mastering the strategies, operational tactics, modern training regimens and logistic support capabilities to begin to formulate a 4th Generation level of operational capability. In East Asia today, the PLA has the dominant forces in space, the air, and very soon, the sea. While this combine of forces is often viewed as "Anti-Access" or "Area Denial" (A2AD) in purpose, China is also gathering regional force projection capabilities. When considering its access to civilian air and sealift, the PLA may have the ability to invade Taiwan early in the next decade and within the next two years, may be able to undertake a rapid amphibious assault against the Senkaku Islands.

Space, C4ISR, missile and regional nuclear forces form the vanguard of China's growing regional capabilities. China now has over 100 satellites in orbit and may soon exceed Russia's number. Nearly 20 optical and radar surveillance satellites, plus an eventual 30+ *Compass* navigation satellites will form the core space portion of a C4ISR (Command, Control, Communication, Computers, Intelligence, Surveillance, Reconnaissance) system that connects "sensors" to "shooters" and allows the PLA to develop new "joint" operations. Ground elements include new Over-the-Horizon (OTH) radar, passive radar and other radar with counter-stealth capabilities. The PLA also operates effective electronic intelligence (ELINT) and signals intelligence (SIGINT) which also assist targeting.

These targeting systems are enabling precision missile and air strikes beyond 1,000km from China, such as by the PLA Second Artillery's much vaunted 1,700km range DF-21D Anti-ship Ballistic Missile (ASBM). Even though there have been no open source reports of a successful test against a moving target, this missile may be operational. After 2015 it may be supplemented by the ASBM version of a new 4,000km range intermediate range ballistic missile (IRBM). The Mach 2-3 speed and 200km range YJ-12 anti-ship missile now arms PLA Naval Air Force (PLANAF) H-6G bombers, which can be cued by PLANAF Y-8J/Searchwater and KJ-200 radar aircraft.

Regional nuclear forces. China also maintains a sizable regional nuclear force. In 2012 retired Russian General Victor Esin, former chief of staff of the Russian Strategic Missile Forces, estimated that the PLA may have up to 700 tactical nuclear warheads for missiles and bombs. Esin estimates there may be as many as 150 tactical nuclear warheads allocated to short range ballistic missiles and land attack cruise missiles.

By 2020 the PLA Air Force (PLAAF) and PLANAF may have close to 1,000 4th Generation and 4+ Generation multirole fighters armed with advanced air-to-air missile and a range of precision guided munitions (PGMs). The 5th Generation Chengdu J-20 may enter service by 2020 and may soon be joined by other 5th Gen types. In 2013 the PLAAF and PLANAF began operating medium altitude/medium endurance (MALE) unmanned aerial vehicles (UAVs), the latter conducting patrols near the Senkakus. The PLA is now developing strategic high-altitude/long-endurance (HALE) UAVs and is testing its first turbofan-powered unmanned combat aerial vehicle (UCAVs) — which eventually will equip future Chinese aircraft carriers.

At sea, the PLA Navy (PLAN) may have over 100 submarines due to their apparent retention of about 30 older Type 033 non-nuclear submarines for training and lesser missions such as mining and Special Operations troop transport. But its modern non-nuclear submarine complement includes about 20 Type 035 *Ming* class, 12 Russian-build *Kilos* armed with the effective Novator *Club* missile family, about 13 indigenous Type 039 *Song* class and 10-12 of the newest Type 039B *Yuan* class, with air independent propulsion (AIP) for longer periods submerged. About 20 *Yuans* are expected to be built. In 2010 the first Type 032 non-nuclear ballistic missile submarine was launched to test new strategic submarine launched ballistic missiles (SLBMs) but this class could be developed to carry ASBMs and multiple types of cruise missiles. The PLAN is expected to acquire about five Type 092 nuclear powered attack submarines (SSNs) before production of the 3rd Generation Type 095 begins.

The PLAN began its aircraft carrier era with the September 2012 commissioning of the *Liaoning,* which in three to four years may reach operational status with an air wing of 24 Shenyang J-15 carrier fighters which are about as effective as the Boeing F/A-18E/F. In the last decade the PLAN has acquired five new types of air-defense capable destroyers. The latest, Type 052D, features a 2nd Generation active phased array radar and launchers for 64 missiles, surface to air, anti-ship and anti-submarine. By 2020 the PLAN's complement of modern combat ships may include 25 destroyers, 40 frigates, 40 corvettes and 80 fast attack craft. While long a weakness, the PLAN's new ships will be increasingly capable of anti-submarine warfare (ASW), aided by new Y-8 based ASW patrol aircraft, powerful sonar array-towing catamaran ships and new bottom-moored sonar sensor networks.

Both formal amphibious and airlift capabilities are also increasing. The PLAN's three 25,000-30,000 ton Type 071 landing platform dock (LPD) amphibious assault ships may be joined by three more, and then by up to six 40,000 ton landing helicopter dock (LHD) assault ships. Existing amphibious lift of LPD and landing ship tank (LST) vessels could allow the PLA to transport about one division of troops and equipment. In May 2013 the PLAN took delivery of its first of four Ukrainian *Zubr* hovercraft, which can carry 500 troops each, or up to 150 tons of equipment, up to speeds of 40 knots. One or two prototypes of the Xian Y-20 heavylift transport are in testing. Eventually it will be able to carry about 65 tons of cargo, comparable to the U.S. C-17.

To exercise strategies short of war China has built up its maritime paramilitary forces. In early 2013 China completed the expected consolidation of seven maritime police and surveillance agencies to form the Chinese Coast Guard. In 2013 this service controls about 43 large patrol ships, but is now in the process of building about 56 more for an eventual total of about 100 ships. These ships are unarmed or lightly-armed, but sufficient for "presence" or "pushing" missions. Where it has none today, the Chinese Coast Guard will soon acquire a new long-range maritime patrol aircraft based on the twin-turboprop Xian MA60, with about a 10 hour endurance, increasing its ability to sustain an aerial presence in contested areas.

Pressuring Japan

China is using both paramilitary and military forces to pressure Japan into making territorial concessions—both in the maritime and air realms. Maritime territorial disputes include differences over their EEZ in the East China Sea, and who has sovereign control over the Senkaku/Daiyou Islands. China is also challenging Japan's Air Defense Identification Zone (ADIZ) as too large for their region. For China, control or neutralization of the Senkakus would undermine the utility of the "First Island Chain" as a means to contain Chinese military power. It is thus ominous that in July 2012, and in May 2013, China's state controlled media allowed commentary that the Ryukyu Island chain, to include Okinawa, belongs to China, not Japan.

In a new book published on 22 October 2013, former Japanese Prime Minister Noda Yoshihiko revealed his government secretly but vigorously sought to defuse a potential crisis with China over the Senkakus by preemptively purchasing the islands to prevent their purchase in an effort led by Tokyo Mayor Ishihara Shintaro. But China shut down secret negotiations and instead of averting a crisis, China used the purchase as an excuse to create one: a campaign of maritime intimidation against Japan that could facilitate a deliberate attack by Chinese forces or lead to an unintended military conflict with Japan.

Through most of 2013, Chinese Coast Guard ships have maintained a near-continuous presence around the 12 nautical mile territorial zone surrounding the Senkakus, and on several occasions (April 2013; 14 September; 27 September; 28 October) they have entered this zone. This has required the Japanese Coast Guard, which has about 121 large patrol ships, to maintain constant multi-ship patrols to meet Chinese incursions, resulting in a strain of Japanese resources. In early October, Japan's Ministry of Defense reported that Japanese Air Self Defense Force (ASDF) fighters had to scramble 149 times against Chinese aircraft in the six months from April to September 2013 – that is almost daily.

China's recent use of a PLANAF BZK-005 UAV, intercepted flying over the Senkakus on 9 September, has sparked a recent military escalation. Given their low cost, about $1 million for a UAV the size of the BZK-005, China could soon inundate Japan's ADIZ with UAVs that might overwhelm the ASDF. On 20 October, Japanese reports indicated that current Prime Minister Abe Shinzo had approved a Defense Ministry plan for shooting down UAVs, which on 26 October a Chinese Defense Ministry spokesman said could be "an act of war." This statement also occurred during the PLAN's "Maneuver-5" exercises, which saw destroyers and frigates pass through the Miyako Strait, and then the PLAN dispatched Y-8J radar aircraft and H-6G bombers through the Miyako Strait, very likely to conduct coordinated combat exercises with PLAN ships.

When the PLAN's *Zubr* large hovercraft enter service, this will add to the temptation for China to strike the Senkakus, as they can carry thousands of troops or hundreds of tons of equipment to these islands in about 4 to 5 hours. An attack on the Sekakus may be quickly followed by attacks on the larger Sakashima Island group just to the south, which has ports and airfields and would better position the PLA to strike Taiwan from an Eastern axis.

Today, it is the ability of 24 Okinawa-based U.S. Marine MV-22 *Osprey* tilt rotor aircraft to put 500 troops or over 100 tons of equipment on these islands in about one hour that provides the margin of deterrence. In response, Japan is considering developing a short-range ballistic missile (SRBM), and is going to assemble its own 3,000 member "Marine" group with up to 20 MV-22s. Japan's army and navy have started amphibious assault exercises with the U.S. Marines-Navy forces. Japan may also have to consider purchasing U.S. F-35B short take-off fighters to equip its larger LHDs or future aircraft carriers.

As there is little chance that Japan will surrender control of the Senkakus or other disputed areas, the optimal outcome may be a Japanese buildup of ISR, missile, fighter and Marine forces to pose an armed deterrent to China, essentially meeting China's militarization of the East China Sea. However, such a buildup may also tempt China to strike before Japan completes its military force expansion.

Continued Preparation for War To Conquer Taiwan

Despite improving relations since the election of President Ma Ying Jeou in 2008, China has not abandoned its goal of controlling Taiwan. This ambition has not waned since Mao's intended 1950 invasion was dissuaded by Josef Stalin, and is motivated by the CCP's intolerance of any competing center of power in the Greater Chinese world -- a matter made more urgent by Taiwan's evolution into an ideologically competitive democracy. While the early part of the previous administration of Chen Shui Bien was marked by Chinese military posturing and threats, recent years have seen an emphasis on political and economic warfare against Taiwan. But China's military preparations to take Taiwan by force have not abated. Beijing would rather intimidate Taipei into "Peace Treaty" that opens the road to submission, but even such a strategy requires that its threats have credibility. And regardless of whether the Kuomintang (KMT) or the Democratic Progressive Party (DPP) wins elections scheduled for 2016, China will be in far stronger position to apply coercive pressures if it so choses.

In addition to ending a major ideological threat to the power position of the CCP, control of Taiwan would also yield spectacular military-strategic benefits. Taiwan sits in the middle of the "First Island Chain" and its immediate access to some of the deepest waters of the Pacific Ocean on its East Coast would be ideal for basing SSBNs. With military forces on Taiwan, the PLA could isolate Japan and South Korea from the Middle Eastern petroleum and sea lanes to global commerce which sustain their economies, forcing them to abandon their alliances with the United States.

In early October 2013, Taiwan's Ministry of National Defense (MND) issued a report estimating that the PLA could achieve "comprehensive military capability to successfully deter any foreign aid that comes to Taiwan's defense by 2020." This statement was reported as meaning that Taiwan's MND assesses that by 2020 the PLA will be able to deter any U.S. attempt to thwart a Chinese attack against Taiwan. The MND report also noted that the PLA is targeting Taiwan with 1,400 missiles. This number could include 400-500 land attack cruise missiles, new types of medium range ballistic missiles (MRBMs) like the DF-16 and the new DF-12 SRBM. The PLA Air Force today has more 4th Generation combat aircraft than does the Taiwan Air Force, and the growing PLA Navy submarine forces is more capable of seeking to blockade Taiwan.

However, from conversations with numerous Taiwanese military officials over the last five years, it is clear that their concern is shifting from threat of blockade to the threat of PLA invasion. The PLA maintains about 300,000 troops in the Taiwan Theater of Operations, but 500,000 may have some experience with amphibious operations. While PLAN formal amphibious lift may only be able to transport one division of troops, the PLA has access to growing lift in dual-use civil large and fast ferries. In 2006 Taiwan's MND estimated the PLA could mobilize 800 ships to transport 5 to 7 infantry divisions. One port, Dalian, may soon have ten new large 20,000 ton to 35,000 ton ferries which in combination could transport up to five armored brigades, including over 600 tanks. Chinese civil airlines, which are integrated into the PLAAF militia structure, could make about 120 large cargo aircraft (mainly Boeings) available for PLA use—about 4x the formal PLA Air Force heavy lift.

PLA ground forces include an estimated 7,000 to 14,000 Special Forces, three divisions of the 15th Airborne Corp (35,000 troops), and two brigades of PLA Navy Marines (12,000 troops), all of which could be used to capture strategic ports and airfields to enable access for follow-on forces. Future regiments of Y-20 transports will be able to lift new wheeled medium-weight armored vehicles, which can also be more easily transported by civilian ferries, and take advantage of Taiwan's excellent road network.

Taiwan's strategic response to China's continued military buildup has been to stress the development of "innovative and asymmetric" capabilities that do not match China's forces but instead target specific elements to maximize deterrence. Despite continued budgetary pressures and the more recent challenge of building an all-volunteer force, this strategy has had bi-partisan support in Taiwan. Perhaps the highest-profile program has been Taiwan's development of "offensive" cruise and ballistic missiles that can more efficiently deter China than can expensive programs like missile defense. Taipei's top procurement priority is to gather technology necessary to build a new class of 1,500 ton submarines. Taipei is also signaling that it would like to purchase the 5th Generation F-35 to eventually replace its 4th Generation F-16s purchased in the early 1990s.

Consolidating Control of the South China Sea

China's decades long effort to establish and then consolidate control over the South China Sea is also motivated in large part by strategic goals. Perhaps the most important strategic goal for China in the South China Sea is to consolidate control over the area within its Nine/Ten Dash Line to ensure that Hainan Island becomes a growing base for global military and space power projection. In the last decade the PLA has built a major new naval base in the Sanya/Yalong Bay area to maintain a future squadron of SSBNs and SSNs and a future aircraft carrier and amphibious assault group. The SSBNs based at Sanya will likely comprise half of the PLA's undersea nuclear missile force, and the carrier-amphibious group will be responsible for projecting power in Southeast Asia, the Indian Ocean, the Persian Gulf, and to Africa. In about two to three years, China will also complete a new space launch center at Wencheng on the Eastern Coast of Hainan, which will be responsible for heavy space launch vehicles. China's future space station, space shuttles, and manned Moon missions of the 2020s will be launched from Wencheng.

China's gradual constriction of the South China Sea has included its taking the Paracel Islands from South Vietnam in 1974, its grabbing reefs in the Spratly Island Group from Vietnam in 1988, and its stealthy occupation of Mischief Reef in late 1994 to early 1995. China now has a useful air and naval base on Woody Island in the Paracel Group, and has built facilities on seven shoals and reefs in the Spratly Group. Periods of aggression have been modulated by periods when Beijing appeared to favor negotiation, but always on a bi-lateral basis to maximize gains, and always rejecting multilateral negotiations with the members of the Association of Southeast Asian Nations (ASEAN). Despite a decade of imploring by ASEAN members, Beijing refuses to sign a Code of Conduct which might impede its consolidation of control.

In June 2009 a then recently-retired PLA Army General, Zhang Li, gave a speech that provided a possible glimpse of China's plans for the South China Sea. He advocated a major buildup of paramilitary and naval ships for enforcing claims in the region—which is now happening. He also proposed a "Three Dimensional Reconnaissance Observation System" of land based radar, aircraft and undersea sensors to better monitor all traffic under, in and over the South China Sea. Finally he called for a new airbase to be built on Mischief Reef, which is 240km from the Philippines, but 1,145km to China's Hainan Island.

In 2012 and 2013, China decided to bear down on the weakest of its competitors, the Philippines. In April and May 2012 Beijing essentially used its paramilitary ships to stand down Manila in a confrontation over control of Scarborough Shoal, which is about 244km from the Philippines and about 900km from China's Hainan Island. China used its ships to deny Philippine ships access to the shoal, which is often used by small fishing vessels as a shelter from poor weather.

Also in 2012 and 2013 China has targeted for harassment a Philippine Navy landing ship, *BRP Sierra Madre*, beached on Second Thomas Shoal in 1999 and used as an outpost manned by Philippine Navy and Marine personnel, about 40km from Chinese-garrisoned Mischief Reef. In July 2012 the PLA Navy briefly beached a frigate on Half Moon Shoal. In August 2012 Philippine military officials on Palawan Island told the author that this beaching was likely in reaction to Philippine interest in exploring for petroleum in this area. But may also have been exercise in pulling a ship off of a reef, as Second Thomas Shoal was only 100km to the North. It appears that through the Summer of 2013 Chinese Coast Guard ships have maintained a vigil at Second Thomas Shoal, seeking to intimidate the Philippines from keeping personnel on the *BRP Sierra Madre*. Should the Philippine military personnel abandon this ship, it is likely that China will drag it off Second Thomas Shoal or destroy it.

What is disturbing is that China's increasing assertiveness against Manila has come at a time when Philippine-U.S. military relations are experiencing a revival from the depths of the early 1990s, following the U.S. departure from Subic Naval Base and Clark Air Base. The last decade has seen a steady increase in U.S. military engagement with Manila, to include counter-insurgency assistance and increasing conventional military training via regular exercises. In early October 2013, had President Barack Obama visited the Philippine as planned, there may have been an agreement which would allow for U.S. forces to again have "rotational", vice permanent, access to Philippine bases. Having largely ignored its needs since the 1980s, Philippine President Benigno Aquino is leading the re-equipment of the Philippine Air Force and Navy for external defense. While the U.S. has so far given Manila two former U.S. Coast Guard frigates, Manila may buy more modern combat ships and small F/A-50 trainer-fighters from South Korea.

As remaining Communist Party-led regimes, Vietnam and China have significant shared interests, but their historic enmity, and more recent conflict in the South China Sea significantly colors their relations. In short, Vietnam also opposes China's effort to assert control over the South China Sea, but in contrast to the Philippines, it is devoting significant resources to building up its South China Sea outposts and its military forces. Later this year the Vietnamese Navy may take delivery of the first of six Russian-built *Kilo* class submarines. Vietnam is on its way to acquiring 44 Russian Su-30 and Su-27 4th Generation fighters, Russian S-300 4th Gen surface-to-air missiles, and Novator *Club* anti-ship missiles.

Building For Power Projection

As stressed in this testimony, one of the key reasons that China is pressing for territorial gains in the East China Sea and South China Sea, and remains focused on conquering Taiwan, is that China's leadership seeks to surmount maritime barriers to its projection of global military power. In late 2004 the CCP began to describe "New Historic Missions" for the PLA, one of which was to increasingly defend the Party's growing international interests. This has included greatly increased participation in United Nations' peacekeeping missions, and the dispatch since December 2008 of 14 naval groups for anti-piracy patrols off of Somalia. Thiss, and an increasing program of naval diplomacy, has seen the PLA Navy establish the beginning of a periodic, if much wider, near-global presence which so far has been largely benign. Even the United States is starting to include China in parts of its large bi-annual RIMPAC exercises.

However, China's goals are not always in concert with the West. As the Libyan Civil War was gathering in 2011, China contemplated sending large quantities of arms to the embattled Muammar Gadaffi. Had the Syrian crisis of September 2013 lasted longer, China may have had the opportunity to send one of its largest ships, a Type 071 LPD, to join Russian forces in tilting against the U.S. and Europe. As China accumulates the means for naval and air projection, it may become more active in defending its radical or authoritarian allied regimes, such as North Korea, Pakistan, Iran, Cuba and perhaps Venezuela.

Today, China fully supports Argentina's claims to the Falklands Islands and is now discussing co-production in Argentina of China's FC-1 fighter, which can be armed with the hypersonic speed CM400AKG anti-ship missile. If conflict were to erupt anew in the next decade, would China send naval forces to support Argentina and counter Britain's expected Navy and Marine deployments?

To project direct military assistance, by the late 2020s the PLA Navy could have a force of four to five aircraft carrier battle groups and up to 12 large amphibious transport-assault ships. China will likely equip its carriers with 5th Gen fighters, capable UCAVs, and may have a short take-off fighter for its LHDs. These battle groups will also include modern escort ships and logistic support ships. By the late 2020s the PLA Air Force could have significant numbers of Y-20 transports and will likely have developed a larger "C-5" size air transport. These will be able to carry light and medium weight mechanized units to distant exercise or battle fields.

Into the 2020s the PLA will also deploy more offensive strategic nuclear missiles and a new missile defense system. The large DF-41 ten-warhead road mobile intercontinental ballistic missile (ICBM) is near deployment. The PLA will also deploy layers of tactical, regional and strategic missile defenses, which when added to China's current estimated 5,000km Underground Great Wall of missile basing and storage facilities, will greatly challenge U.S. nuclear deterrence calculations. By the 2020s the PLA will control a large dual-use space station, a dual-use space shuttle, and very likely have a dual-use Moon Base -- all in order to expand China's ability to deny and control access to outer space.

Conclusion

Again, while the Obama Administration has earned deserved praise for its Rebalance to Asia "pivot" policy, a new momentum set in 2011 and 2012 of improving and tightening Asian alliance relations could be undermined by the fiscal uncertainty that may prevent the U.S. from preserving and building upon its position in Asia. In addition to the conspicuous absence of President Obama from an important Asian diplomatic schedule in early October, the Department of Defense has had to cut back on important bi-lateral and multilateral exercise activity with Asian partners in 2013. Adding to uncertainty are suggestions from the Department of Defense that sequestration may force a reduction to 8 U.S. Navy carrier battle groups and the elimination of whole types of aircraft from the U.S. Air Force, including the A-10 ground support fighter and the KC-10 aerial tanker. In addition, there are new doubts about whether the U.S. can afford critical future developments such as an effective UCAV, or a new nuclear attack submarine missile module extension, both for the U.S. Navy.

In 2010 the Administration learned the hard way that it had to stand up to China's pressure and did so on the Korean Peninsula and in Southeast Asia. But it also became clear that new military strategies and capabilities must be pursued to counter quickly-emerging Chinese A2AD capabilities. If Washington is to sustain a leadership role in deterring pressure now, and perhaps aggression later from China, it must demonstrate that determination by regularly identifying Chinese threatening behavior, be it the East China Sea, Taiwan Strait and South China Sea. It must be stated that China's behavior is increasing the chances for military incidents and that the U.S. will defend its allies if they are attacked. Washington must also back that determination by leading an Asian military coalition with modern U.S. forces at its core.

This is simply not the time for the United States to be considering additional reductions in its nuclear forces or in its principle power projection capabilities. Instead the U.S. should reintroduce secure tactical nuclear weapons on its submarines. It is essential that the U.S. join with Japan and others to build an Asian regional ISR network that provides all partners with a far better real-time picture of Chinese military activities. It is also critical that the U.S. develop new classes of missiles, from short- to intermediate-range, to target Chinese Naval forces as a means of deterring aggression. Many of these missiles should be offered to allies facing Chinese pressure, like Japan and the Philippines. It is also critical to help Taiwan build new asymmetric military capabilities that can target PLA invasion forces and have a better chance of sustaining deterrence on the Taiwan Strait.

Mr. ROHRABACHER. Thank you very much for that testimony. We now have Steven Mosher, director of the Population Research Institute. And, again, all of our witnesses have lengthy resumes that will be included in the record.

Go right ahead, Mr. Mosher.

STATEMENT OF MR. STEVEN MOSHER, DIRECTOR, POPULATION RESEARCH INSTITUTE

Mr. MOSHER. Well, I commend the chairman, Chairman Rohrabacher and Ranking Member Keating, for holding this timely hearing. As Rick just mentioned, there have recently been renewed incursions by Chinese assets into Japanese territorial waters around the Senkakus and the Ryukyus in general, and I would note that a top Chinese general has actually questioned the legitimacy of Japanese claims, not just to the tiny Senkakus but to the entire Ryukyu Island chain, including Okinawa with its U.S. military bases. And knowing the situation in China, knowing that people rarely speak out of turn without being punished, I take such warnings, such suggestions by Chinese generals as tantamount to diplomatic announcements.

Seemingly, everywhere we look, we see evidence of China's increasing aggressiveness. And I think it is past time to ask. I think, as the former Secretary of Defense Donald Rumsfeld did many years ago, why this ongoing military buildup when China faces no external threat? Why these provocative acts? What, after all, does China want? I think to suggest that Australia somehow poses a military threat to China is vastly overstating rather underpopulated Australia's desire to defend its own territorial waters from a country which now is in the process of trying to annex the entire South China Sea, which is a territorial claim roughly equivalent to as if Nazi Germany had declared before the outset of the conflict in World War II that it owned the entire Mediterranean. I mean, it is an extraordinary territorial claim.

In May this year, Chinese troops intruded nearly 12 miles into Indian territory. It withdrew only after India agreed to withdraw its own troops from the area. And so this high-altitude border dispute continues to simmer. The Indian Prime Minister is going to China, to Beijing, in a couple of days, apparently to sign a border cooperation agreement on Chinese terms, which I believe is what one Indian analyst called an exercise in course of military diplomacy, or bullying in short.

China is sowing new seeds of conflict by continuing to expand its military presence in the South China Sea, where I know, Mr. Chairman, you have been personally. Last year, it seized the Scarborough Shoal, which lies off the coast of the Philippines, by force. When the Philippines protested, the PRC reacted by saying that the Philippines' claims were illegal and that it would never agree to international arbitrary over the shoal or any other claims. Now, that is important because the Philippines is now seeking U.N. assistance against China. And we, at least the current administration, seem to be extremely reluctant to back U.S. allies in the face of Chinese aggression. We have only said in the person of U.S. Secretary of State John Kerry that all countries have a right to seek arbitration to resolve competing territorial claims. We have not vigorously backed the obvious claim of the Philippines to territory which lies very close to its own homeland.

I see China's behavior as reflecting something fundamental about the Chinese Party state. A government that rules its own people by brute force—we all remember Tiananmen—is naturally inclined to treat its smaller, weaker neighbors the same way, especially if they were, as in the past, tributary states of China. I think this accounts, in part, for the palpable disdain with which it treats the other claimants in the South China Sea dispute, including Vietnam and the Philippines, both of which have stronger claims for the Spratlies and Paracels than does China itself.

I would also add to the death toll that you, Mr. Chairman, mentioned at the outset of this hearing in your remarks, to the death toll caused by the one-party dictatorship that rules China, we must add the 400 million eliminated by China's infamous one-child policy. I was an eyewitness to women being arrested and forced to be aborted at 7, 8, and 9 months of pregnancy in China in 1980. And those atrocities, those kinds of atrocities still continue today.

Only the continued presence of U.S. assets, the U.S. Seventh Fleet in the Far East, stays China's hand. China has actually suggested that we withdraw to Hawaii and cede everything west of Hawaii to China. There is little doubt if that happened that China would then occupy the remaining islands in the South China Sea by force, ejecting the garrisons of other nations, and begin to demand the ships transiting its ''interior waters'' would first seek permission to do so or run the risk of being boarded and quarantined. This is actually now the official policy of the Chinese Government as of last November. Beijing announced last November that Chinese authorities will board and seize control of foreign ships that ''illegally enter'' the area that he claims is part of the Province of Henan. That is the entire area inside the 9-line.

Now, seizing ships in international waters is an act of war under international law. I believe that China has been clear about its intentions in this regard.

We could talk about continued double digit increases in the PLA's budget. We could talk about other new capabilities. But I am really less worried about China's capabilities than its intentions. I am concerned that China, which lacks transparency in terms of its military budget and in stating its intentions, is only emboldened by our careful and measured and nuanced and oftentimes too quiet response to acts of aggression. I think that emboldens the Chinese leadership and open society relies on comprehensive and accurate information to inform both its citizens and its allies of the common threats that they face.

I believe we need another commission. And I realize there are a couple of commissions that serve to alert us to happenings in China now. But I believe we need another commission that focuses specifically on China's intentions. There is a precedent for that. I served on the U.S. Commission on Broadcasting for the PRC back in the '90s, which specifically looked at the question of whether or not we needed a radio-free broadcast system broadcasting into China news and information that was denied the Chinese people themselves by their state-censored media. The answer that we on the commission reached was yes, we did need such a broadcasting service. And it does yeoman work today.

I believe we need another commission to look specifically at China's intentions. It would review; evaluate; and, if necessary, correct any understatements that are reached by other intelligence agencies. Such a check on the current administration consensus on China would be invaluable. Such reviews proved to be such during the Soviet era when a number of independent commissions reviewed Soviet military capabilities and intentions. This way we can get a timely, independent assessment of China's military intentions because in a few years, it will have the hardware it needs to undertake aggression, both in Asia and in different parts of the world. It is vital that we understand now before it gets that hardware how they intend to use it.

Thank you.

[The prepared statement of Mr. Mosher follows:]

What Does China Want?

Why, as China grows more powerful, does it become more bellicose?

by Steven W. Mosher

Testimony submitted for a Hearing on

"China's Maritime and other Geographic Threats"

to be held before the

Subcommittee on Europe, Eurasia, and Emerging Threats

10:00 a.m. on Wednesday,
October 30, 2013,
Room 2255, Rayburn House Office Building.

I commend the Chairman for this timely hearing. Less than 48 hours ago, Chinese vessels recklessly entered Japanese territorial waters around the Senkaku Islands. Seemingly everywhere we look, we see evidence of China's increasing aggressiveness and it is past time to ask, Why this ongoing military buildup when China faces no external threat? Why these provocative acts? What, after all, does China want?.

Since last September, China has been vigorously asserting its new--and historically groundless--claim to the Senkaku Islands by sending a constant stream of naval vessels and planes to harass Japanese patrol boats there. The most recent such encounter, as I mentioned, occurred a mere two days ago. No only that, but a top Chinese general has questioned the legitimacy of Japanese claims not just to the tiny Senkakus, but to the entire Ryukyu Island chain, including Okinawa with its U.S. military bases.

Then in May, Chinese troops intruded nearly 12 miles into Indian territory, withdrawing only after India agreed to withdraw its own troops from the area. The high-altitude frontier dispute, which has been simmering since the Sino-Indian War of 1962, involves territory the size of Greece with a population of over a million. India is apparently prepared to sign a border cooperation agreement on Chinese terms, an exercise in coercive military diplomacy that Brahma Chellaney, an Indian analyst, calls bullying.

And then there is the South China Sea, where China has been aggressively asserting its sovereignty over the 1.4 million-square-mile stretch of open ocean. Last November, Beijing announced that Chinese authorities will board and seize control of foreign ships that "illegally enter" the area that it claims is part of the province of Hainan. Seizing ships in international waters is an act of war under international law.

China has also sowed new seeds of conflict by continuing to expand its military presence in the area. Last year it seized the Scarborough Shoal, which lies off the coast of the Philippines, by force. When that country protested, the PRC reacted by saying that the Philippines' claims were illegal, and that it would never agree to international arbitration over the Shoal or any other claims. In January it issued a new map that, for the first time, precisely delineates its grandiose new claim. What is shows is the largest attempted land grab since the Second World War. It is rather as if Nazi Germany had claimed the entire Mediterranean Sea as sovereign territory.

And so it goes. Nearly every month China is making a new territorial claim or bullying its neighbors over an existing one. Worse yet, it is defining these new claims, like its longstanding claims to Taiwan, Tibet and Xinjiang, as "core interests," vital to national survival and are emphatically *not* up for negotiation.

The Obama administration has proven extremely reluctant to back U.S. allies in the face of such Chinese aggression. U.S. Secretary of State John Kerry, for example, offered only tacit backing to the Philippines' efforts to seek UN assistance against China, saying only that all countries had a right to seek arbitration to resolve competing territorial claims. Perhaps they had imagined that China's opening to the West would result in a modernizing, democratizing China that would willingly take its place in the existing international system. A younger, foreign-educated leadership would renounce force in favor of negotiation. The kinds of armed conflict that marred the PRC's first three decades would be a thing of the past, and any remaining territorial disputes would be resolved peaceably.

But China's integration into the world economy has apparently not defanged the Chinese Party-State, nor led it, metaphorically speaking, to beat its swords into plowshares. Instead, it is taking the money that it has made from selling cheap, state-subsidized "plowshares" around the world and using it to make "swords," which it is now brandishing with increasing frequency.

I see China's behavior as reflecting something fundamental about the nature of the Chinese Party-State. A government that rules its own people by brute force--remember Tiananmen--is naturally inclined to treat its smaller, weaker neighbors the same way. Especially if they were, in the past, tributary states. This accounts in part for the palpable distain with which it treats the other claimants in the South China Sea dispute, including Vietnam and The Philippines, both of which have stronger claims to the Spratlys and Paracels than does China itself.

Only the continued presence of the U.S. Seventh Fleet in the Far East stays China's hand. Were that force to be withdrawn to Hawaii, as China has suggested, there is little doubt that China would then occupy the remaining islands in the South China Sea by force, ejecting the garrisons of other nations, and begin to demand that ships transiting its "interior waters" first seek permission to do so or run the risk of being boarded and quarantined.

Deng Xiaoping once advised his immediate successors, who ruled a much weaker China, to "bide your time and hide your capabilities." But that was then. Now China capabilities are on track to approach parity with the U.S. in the Pacific theater in a few years, and already far, far exceed those of all of its nearest maritime neighbors except Japan.

Continuing double-digit increases in the PLA's budget are fueling China's military buildup. While the exact amount that China spends on its military is unclear, what is obvious is that the more funding the PLA receives, the sooner it will achieve parity with the U.S. military. China is building a nuclear arsenal, along with a range of delivery systems, that could match or even exceed that of the United States in the coming decades. A blue water navy, along with components of China's first indigenously produced aircarft carrier, is under construction, and naval bases in Burma, Pakistan, and Sri Lanka will enable its resupply. As the latest Pentagon report confirms, China already "has the largest force of major combatants, submarines, and amphibious warfare ships in Asia." Moreover, China is constructing its own GPS satellite network, has developed a ground-launched anti-satellite missile to improve its counter-space capabilities, and is building the Shenlong spaceplane with advanced propulsion characteristics for possible military use.

Emboldened by their new capabilities, and firmly in control of the Chinese polity, the next generation of Chinese leaders have apparently decided that it it no longer has to bide its time although it still prefers to hide its capabilities.

I have long believed that the Chinese leadership holds an expansive view of Chinaese place in the world, and that it is interested in reestablishing its historical role as the Hegemon of Asia. It is imperative that we educate the American people in this regard.

An open society relies on comprehensive and accurate information to inform both its citizens and its allies of the common threats that they face. The annual *Pentagon Report on Chinese Military Developments* does not go far enough in this regard. In a time of economic uncertainty, and in the face of an ongoing Chinese military build-up, it is especially important that U.S. taxpayers understand the importance maintaining both a quantitative and qualitative lead in military capabilities over China. It is equally important that allied and friendly governments, along with their citizens, be informed of military developments in China. China needs to know that its continuing military buildup has not gone unnoticed, and that the U.S. and its allies are well aware of its larger designs.

Ascertaining both China's capabilities and its intentions is critical. I therefore recommend that the U.S. Congress establish a commission to review, evaluate and, if necessary, correct any shortcomings in the Pentagon Report. Such a "check" on the current administration consensus on China would be invaluable, as such reviews proved to be during the Soviet era when a number of independent commissions reviewed Soviet military capabilities and intentions.

Such a review would be a timely and substantive way to get an independent, overall assessment of China's military development. The public hearings that it would hold, not less than its annual report, would add to the constructive debate over China's intentions, as continues to engineer double digit increases in its military budget, and develop specific capabilities that not only put U.S. allies and assets in Asia at risk, but the American homeland as well.

———————

Mr. ROHRABACHER. I would like to thank all of my witnesses, all of our witnesses, today. And what we will have now is just some questions and answers. All right. And that is good. All right. As my staff recommends, I would suggest that I would like—well, first of all, let me just note this for the record. Our subcommittee focuses on Europe and Asia, central Asia, but it also in its definition talks about emerging threats.

That is why we are here today. This is part of a discussion on what some of us believe is an emerging threat to the peace of the world and the security of the United States of America. And from the witnesses today, I would say we do have one voice of disagreement. And we will get into that discussion. And we are very happy to have you with us to promote that type of discussion because, of course, in countries like China, they don't have people on the other side of issues where they are being discussed, the other side of issues that the state has taken a stand on.

I would like to ask the panel very quickly if you might mention any specific weapons systems that China is building that threatens America's naval or air or space assets. And maybe just go down the line just very quickly. Dr. Pickert, can you think of a weapons system that they are developing that you might warn us against?

Mr. PICKERT. I think specifically the sea power aspect is under the envelope of strategic conventional weapons. And the East Wind system of—these are essentially huge SCUD missiles that can operate from the bases in China to essentially any of these things which are being disputed can be blown off the face of the Earth without even leaving China.

Mr. ROHRABACHER. Are they accurate enough to be——

Mr. PICKERT. They don't have to be accurate. You just shoot 20 of them, and they will knock off a whole corner of the universe. I don't know if you have ever seen an arc-light strike by B–52s, they take out a whole grid square of territory. This is a SCUD tactic. It is using mass attack on a particular place. And you have 20 missiles, all shooting at the same thing. And these islands are in specific areas where you have naval forces are simply deterred from using that space if it escalates to anything beyond local conflict. And the trouble with each of these areas is they cannot be held as territory because they can be obliterated.

Mr. ROHRABACHER. Mr. Fisher?

Mr. FISHER. Mr. Chairman, I would call to your attention the system of weapons that the Chinese are developing and beginning to deploy, starting with a dual-use space program, both manned and unmanned, that provides targeting and communications and data links for missiles, like the anti-ship ballistic missile, new supersonic anti-ship missiles that are being carried today by Chinese bombers, future hypersonic anti-ship missiles, not to mention what they will be putting on their aircraft carrier. As soon as that starts service in about 2 to 3 years, it will have a fighter that is about as good as our F–18 Super Hornet. And submarines are being built like dumplings. And they are good, and they have air-independent propulsion so that they can stay underwater for a long time.

And this is just what is going to be hitting us in Asia. In the next decade, China will have the wherewithal to project force around the world, both mechanized airborne and mechanized amphibious infantry supported by aircraft carriers and an even more robust space architecture.

Mr. ROHRABACHER. Mr. Mosher?

Mr. MOSHER. Well, I believe Mr. Fisher has hit on the key points here. And I would just say that China has rapidly upgraded the capabilities of its navy. And it has now a navy the largest force of major combatant submarines and amphibious warfare ships in Asia. And many of them are first-rate. China is constructing its own GPS satellite network. It has a ground-launched anti-satellite capability capable of taking out our communications satellites and is developing a space plane, the Shunlong, which may have military capabilities.

Mr. ROHRABACHER. Here is your chance.

Mr. SANDBY-THOMAS. Sure.

Mr. ROHRABACHER. Are these not a threat, Dr. Thomas?

Mr. SANDBY-THOMAS. Well, I think they are fairly comprehensive. I think the big concern is, sort of as I noted, the guided missile destroyers in terms of how that impacts U.S. Navy operations, particularly for providing support, whether they could take out aircraft carriers. But some of it seems to be developing or being developed, probably close to production. I am not entirely clear.

Mr. ROHRABACHER. Let me just note that one of the sad aspects of the answers that we just got is that the source of research and development for many of the weapons systems that you are talking about are the American taxpayers. I mean, many of the weapons systems that China is developing are based on information that they have stolen and hacked and gotten from American industry. And sometimes they have actually stolen from our own Government operations. Is there any doubt about that? Can we comment on that? Yes, sir?

Mr. FISHER. Acquisition of foreign technology is essential to the Chinese military research and development process. From the opening of our relations with China, Mr. Chairman, China has deployed tens of thousands of engineering students to the United States to study at our best schools and largely for the purpose of taking that information and experience back to China to apply to weapons programs. I can offer numerous citations of experts that work for NASA, went back to China, and are now helping to develop space planes, which will be used for military purposes.

When China was developing its current fourth generation fighter, the J–10, it had to develop new composite materials for the air frame. It actually came to California and had those composites validated by an American company. It went back to China and put them into production. They work very fine. Thank you very much.

Mr. ROHRABACHER. I think that says it all. Thank you very much.

Mr. Keating?

Mr. KEATING. Thank you, Mr. Chairman. Given our focus as a committee on Europe—and Mr. Fisher referenced NATO—I would just like to know how our European partners are responding to the recent developments in Asia. And should we be asking them to do more? And if so, what do you think the contributions they could bring might be?

Mr. FISHER. Mr. Keating, it is a very important question. For 20 years, the United States Government has been engaged with our European allies over the issue of arms sales to China. The European Union established an embargo, as did the United States, after the Tiananmen massacre. The Europeans have, unfortunately, defined and redefined their embargo to allow more and more dual-use technology to go to China. And this is going directly in the People's Liberation Army.

Eurocopter, for example, has a new full-up helicopter co-development program, to include the engine with the Chinese helicopter industry. This will be a new modern, state-of-the-art 6- to 7-ton helicopter. The Europeans tell me when I see them at numerous arms shows that no, this helicopter will never go into the PLA. But every other European helicopter that the Chinese have co-produced—and there are about four or five of them—they have all gone into the military. And naval engines, all Chinese non-nuclear submarines and new combatant ships use European-designed naval engines, large German-designed engines.

I just found a citation a few weeks ago that the Chinese ship-building industry has purchased a state-of-the-art Spanish ship design three-dimensional software. And this is already helping the Chinese to develop better combat ships.

When we find these examples, we should be quite insistent with our allies that this is not helpful, that this is actually creating problems for them because the sooner that China has the ability to wage war against Taiwan, which it is still building tremendously to conquer Taiwan, perhaps early in the next decade, attack Japan over the Senkaku/Diaoyu Islands, or enforce its outrageous and expansive claims in the South China Sea. Those could all possibly engage American forces in support of allies and detract, either in the short term or very likely also in the long term, to assist our European allies from threats that are growing against them as well.

Mr. KEATING. So you mentioned that there might be compromise because of their sales. When you gave your address, was there any concern from any of those countries about what was occurring through China's actions?

Mr. FISHER. Oh, yes, a great concern, many questions. And the information that I was giving, surprisingly, was viewed as new. Many of the parliamentarians from our NATO ally countries who attended this conference simply did not have an understanding that China was at a point where it was threatening to start and cause wars.

Our annual PLA military power report that the Pentagon has been issuing since early in the last decade really needs to be translated into multiple languages. It needs to be upgraded. It needs to be published as a book with pictures and charts. Yes, that may look like the old Soviet military power report of the 1980s, but that is what our friends and our allies are looking for from the United States. We have to identify these threats in order to ask and encourage our allies to take them seriously and then respond appropriately.

Mr. KEATING. And I think all of our panel has addressed this in one way or another, but just to have a concise, you know, answer to this, if I could just go across our panel and just ask, how immediate is the threat for the China's maritime and territorial disputes? And could you just, you know, in very short language describe it as either short, medium-term risk of armed conflict? What is the time frame and how real is it, if we could just quickly go? I just want to zero in on that.

Mr. PICKERT. I will start at this end by saying that all of these disputes are essentially traps for points of opportunity for regional and local conflicts, one on one with small countries that cannot respond to them.

Mr. KEATING. So short, medium?

Mr. PICKERT. That is present right now all over the place. It is happening every day. And their strategic overview of that is to protect, to make sure that we do not interfere in that process.

Mr. KEATING. Mr. Fisher?

Mr. FISHER. In the last 3 weeks, Japan has threatened to shoot down Chinese unmanned aircraft that would violate Japanese air space. A Chinese unmanned aircraft basically did that in early September, and it was intercepted. The Chinese have responded just this past weekend that the shoot-down of a UAV by Japan would be an act of war. This act of war could actually transpire at almost any time, Congressman.

Mr. KEATING. Short-term. Mr. Mosher?

Mr. MOSHER. The threat is immediate and ongoing. That is why Japan is building now its own brain expeditionary force to protect the Senkaku Islands and also the Ryukyus. It never felt the need of doing that before. It does now. So Japan feels an immediate threat. It is in the neighborhood. And I think we ought to look to Japan's response to calibrate our own.

Mr. KEATING. Mr. Sandby-Thomas?

Mr. SANDBY-THOMAS. Yes. I would think the likelihood of conflict is higher now than, say, it was a year ago. In terms of immediacy, it seems that the potential for provocation on both sides is there, but I still don't think that war will break out, I guess.

Mr. KEATING. No, but there is consensus among all four of you that there could be conflict in the short-term that is escalating. And that is an interesting point that we should bear in mind and seek out our Europe allies and our partners in Europe so that there is better understanding of that. So I thank you very much. That was very helpful.

And for the purpose of the rest of the hearing, Representative Lowenthal will be assuming the ranking membership. And I thank him for doing that and thank you because I think that last series of things put a time frame on some of the urgency of what we are facing.

Thank you.

Mr. ROHRABACHER. And thank you very much.

And, Mr. Lowenthal, who represents the district next to my district in Southern California and he also now represents a city that includes the Ports of Los Angeles and Long Beach. And these ports, of course, tie us to China. And events in China are very significant to Southern Californians. And we welcome his participation today.

Mr. LOWENTHAL. Thank you. Thank you, Mr. Chair. I do agree that we have figured out ways between you and I to settle our disputes peacefully, not that we have that many.

I just want to follow up on that last question about, really, the level of tension in terms of the maritime disputes and what really specifically at this moment should be the U.S. role. And I would like to start with Mr. Sandby-Thomas and then ask all of the panel, what now? Where do we go now for the United States in terms of this? If tensions have escalated, what specifically should we be doing today besides holding this hearing and learning about what is really going on and not denying the existence of the problems that are going on?

Mr. SANDBY-THOMAS. Well, in terms of the East China Sea disputes, it is unclear necessarily an unsafe China strategy, but obviously there is this issue of energy around the islands. I think the islands in and of themselves don't really hold a huge amount of value. They are sure these barren rocks are uninhabitable.

Mr. LOWENTHAL. Right.

Mr. SANDBY-THOMAS. So there is energy, but that seems that that could be something of joint negotiation. There have been negotiations in the past. We jointly developed these. So that could be resumed.

In terms of the Chinese position, it seems that the decision by the Japanese Government to purchase the islands may be, on the one hand, sort of changed how the islands are administered but, on the other hand, maybe indicated that Japan was—it kind of changed the status quo. And so the Chinese actions in that context, maybe I think they have a strategic value. If the Senkaku Islands weren't part of this first island chain, the Chinese incursion seems to be sort of testing Japanese resolve on this. I think they are testing both Japanese resolve, how far can China get, can it kind of break this chain, does it have an opportunity to do so, and how strong is the resolve between the U.S. and Japan. So would the U.S. defend Japan if there were a sort of conflict with the breakout?

I think on the latter part, the U.S. has reiterated its obligations under the U.S.-Japan Security Treaty. So that seems fairly clear. The difficulty really resides in sort of the Japanese and the Chinese. And they have various competing sort of interests and aims. They have different audiences that they are playing to. Sort of obviously in terms of, say, Chinese domestic politics, negotiation with Japan is not so easy. And, particularly, I think some of the politicians in their statements have linked the Senkaku Island back to sort of Japan's sort of wartime actions within China.

And on the Japanese side, it seemingly is the China threat is being sort of amplified to sort of push forward demands for increases in naval capability. So I think that is what contributes to the volatility.

In terms of the U.S., I think it has sort of gone as far as it can. You know, I am not sure that it—I think, you know, it is important to indicate that the U.S. would intervene. And, you know, the likelihood of conflict I think is an immediate threat, but I wouldn't expect conflict to break other than through the sort of accidental issue. I don't think the intention of either side is to engage in conflict, but that is something that could change, hopefully, going forward.

Mr. MOSHER. Well, I would have to disagree, at least in part, with that assessment. I believe that China's leaders since Tiananmen massacre have deliberately stoked patriotism. They installed in the early '90s a patriotic education program in the schools. So that from kindergarten through college, the Chinese history textbooks are full of great Chinese Shogunist sentiments, talking about how China was once a great nation and will be again, how the Japanese, who are called in colloquial parlance in China "dwarf barbarians," which is not a happy phrase, have periodically invaded and ravaged China. And they use this anti-Japanese sentiment in order to reinforce their own control over China. The appeal of communism in China has long vanished, but the appeal of patriotism still has a strong hold on the Chinese people.

So, in part, these aggressive acts enable the Chinese leadership to say to the Chinese people, "We are in the process of building a great and glorious China, equivalent to those in the Song, the Tang, the Ming dynasty." You see how we are asserting Chinese rights overseas in the Senkakus and the South China Sea and elsewhere. We are going to bring these tributary states to heal.

I happen to believe that without the calming presence of U.S. assets in Asia, that Chinese open aggression would have already occurred vis-à-vis the Philippines, for example, last year in Scarborough Shoal. Were it not for the possibility of U.S. intervention, the Chinese might well have sank the Philippine patrol boats. Instead, they drove them off a water cannon.

Last year they cut the towed sonar arrays of Vietnamese survey vessels. They were trying to survey waters immediately off Vietnam's coast, but that is part of the extraordinary territorial claim made by China. They cut the survey cables and drove the Vietnamese ships back to port. They might have behaved even more aggressively were they not worried about the possibility of the U.S. intervention. The same thing with regard to their last November claim that they had the right to intercept, interdict, and board ships in the South China Sea. We guarantee freedom of the seas, freedom of navigation. And as long as the U.S. remains engaged in Asia and reassures its allies that we will be there in the event of conflict, China gets that message loud and clear.

So I think for us to equivocate or not state clearly what our position is encourages aggression and that, as in the 1880s, when we faced a different kind of threat, we can achieve peace in Asia through strength but certainly not by telegraphing weakness.

Mr. FISHER. Congressman, I would like to answer your question by also saying that if we do nothing today, then we risk the danger in the short term of having our allies possibly defeated in skirmishes around Senkakus, in the South China Sea, but that this is simply unacceptable. If our allies are undermined, if they lose confidence in their alliances with the United States, they have alternatives. And in my opinion, they will develop their own nuclear missiles, Japan perhaps, followed by South Korea, followed by Vietnam and Australia. It could happen rather quickly. And after that, the prospect of a skirmish, being one that escalates to a nuclear exchange that we are drawn into, is real.

So, sir, I would suggest that, as Steven suggests, we have to be very clear to the Chinese about what we consider unacceptable behavior. And we have to support our friends and allies. We have to make clear that we are there to back up our alliances, that we are there to support our longstanding friendship with Taiwan by selling them the systems that they need to deter war because if we fail to do this, we are, as Steven, I would agree completely, inviting conflict. And those conflicts very well could consume our own.

Thank you.

Mr. PICKERT. Well, I think the most important thing is to maintain relationships over a long period of time with the peripheral states, especially ASEAN in this case, because that was developed as a counter-alliance to China almost 50 years ago and still is. The problem is our relationships bilaterally with those countries are not really integrated into a comprehensive strategy. They are only one-on-one meetings, photo ops at a certain time wearing some kind of ridiculous outfit in a photo op. Our relationships have to go beyond that into long-range ties with the countries, which, especially in the cases where we don't have those ties, like Vietnam, it is important to build them. And in places where we have had long ones and are essentially neglecting them now, such as with Thailand, which is a very big and important country, cutting back on our military relations, which I know we are doing, is a bad, bad sign. And, therefore, we should spend a little money on the relationships as more important than hardware, which is essentially really checkmated by the strategic missile systems that are being built.

Mr. ROHRABACHER. Well, thank you very much. I thank our witnesses today and my colleagues. I will just do a summary. And then we will bring this to an end.

Let me just—we live in a changing world. This is a very changing world. My father flew the first DC–3s into Shanghai in the final months of the Second World War. And he always told me how he was sent there from the Philippines, where they have been flying up and down from the Philippines. And when they landed, their job was to make sure that that airport was available so that we could now have input into Shanghai, which had been under Japanese occupation. And things had broken down there. And so they were sent in. And when he got to Shanghai with a number of DC–3s and filled with Marines and equipment, set up communications, et cetera, an American presence in that city, the first thing he did was get off the airplane and grabbed what appeared to be a Chinese official or someone who knew what was going on and said, "Where is the home of the Japanese commanding officer?"

And he said, "Oh, it is a big house over there."

And then my father lined up his Marines and marched up to the house and knocked on the door. An older man, Japanese man, answered the door. And my father said, "This house is now being confiscated by the United States Marine Corps. You will vacate within ½ hour and not come back." My father was 24 years old, had never been out of North Dakota before World War II. It is the kind of influence that we were exercising throughout the world.

And I saw a thing about last night I was up watching a documentary on the Battle of the Bulge. And he had all of these 18- and 19-year-old Americans. They were facing the German Army. And America since that time period has spread out from the heartland of our country to be this huge force in the world. We no longer have that ability. We no longer can afford to be the dominant force in the planet militarily. We don't have the capability of having our young men go to a foreign country and knock on the door and tell the aggressor to get out of the building or to send 18- and 19-year-olds as cannon fodder to stop an invasion by a totalitarian force in Europe.

We were mentioning we are not spending as much money. Well, if we do, we have to borrow it from China in order to spend it. What does that tell you? The world is a changing situation. We have to come up with a strategy that works to promote peace in the world and also freedom in the world, which I believe peace and freedom go together. They are two sides of the same coin. And that is why we need to talk about these serious challenges. And I believe that as we develop a strategy for the future, we have to understand the threat in Asia and the threat that China plays to our planet, first to the Pacific and to our planet.

The testimony we had today on the expansion of Chinese missile and space power; the expansion of the submarine fleet, Chinese submarine fleet; and the utilization of Chinese air power expanding by utilizing Western technology, perhaps Argentineans, et cetera, this means that we have a challenge, but at the same time, we have our limitations. All of this has to be put into given a lot more thought, given a lot more discussion, as we have had today.

Let me just note that when I hear that the Germans are working with the Chinese to develop certain weapons systems, I can't help but not be so upset that some of our people might be listening in to the German Government's conversations. I know Mrs. Merkel may not like to hear that, but the fact is that our intelligence systems need to keep us informed of the development of this type of threat.

And, finally, let me just say we don't live in a world where a 24-year-old young man goes and confronts a Japanese general who is engaged in an aggressive act in China. We live in a world, instead, that you have an aggressive posturing by China and a bullying of its neighbors by a government in Beijing that is the world's worst human rights abuser.

I think the most important statement made in today's hearing was that a country, a government that so tortures its own people, so represses them and murders them, how can we expect them to treat other neighboring weak countries any better than they treat their own people? And if that does not forbode us or to warn us, what does? The fact is the way they treat their own people, they will treat the rest of the world.

And Japan, we need to make sure Japan, which can be a very positive force, that we need to not be afraid of Japan anymore. We need to make sure that where we cannot afford to balance off this expansion of Chinese power and military power in the Pacific, we can't afford that, but we can afford to work with Japan, who with their contribution can help balance off that shift in power and, thus, help ensure the peace of the world. We should be working with the Japanese for that end.

With that said, this hearing is now adjourned.

[Whereupon, at 11:39 a.m., the subcommittee was adjourned.]

APPENDIX

MATERIAL SUBMITTED FOR THE HEARING RECORD

SUBCOMMITTEE HEARING NOTICE
COMMITTEE ON FOREIGN AFFAIRS
U.S. HOUSE OF REPRESENTATIVES
WASHINGTON, D.C. 20515-6128

Subcommittee on Europe, Eurasia, and Emerging Threats
Dana Rohrabacher (R-CA), Chairman

October 28, 2013

TO: MEMBERS OF THE COMMITTEE ON FOREIGN AFFAIRS

You are respectfully requested to attend an OPEN hearing of the Committee on Foreign Affairs to be held by the Subcommittee on Europe, Eurasia and Emerging Threats in Room 2255 of the Rayburn House Office Building (and available on the Committee website at www.foreignaffairs.gov):

DATE: Wednesday, October 30, 2013

TIME: 10:00 a.m.

SUBJECT: China's Maritime and other Geographic Threats

WITNESSES: Perry Pickert, Ph.D.
                   Retired Career Intelligence Officer

                   Mr. Rick Fisher
                   Senior Fellow
                   Asian Military Affairs
                   International Assessment and Strategy Center

                   Mr. Steven Mosher
                   Director
                   Population Research Institute

                   Peter Sandby-Thomas, Ph.D.
                   Visiting Lecturer of Political Science
                   University of Massachusetts Dartmouth

By Direction of the Chairman

COMMITTEE ON FOREIGN AFFAIRS

MINUTES OF SUBCOMMITTEE ON _____ *Europe, Eurasia, and Emerging Threats* _____ HEARING

Day___*Wednesday*___Date_____*10/30/2013*_____Room___*2255 Rayburn*___

Starting Time ___*10:10AM*___Ending Time ___*11:39AM*___

Recesses |_____| (____to ____) (____to ____) (____to ____) (____to ____) (____to ____) (____to ____)

Presiding Member(s)

Chairman Dana Rohrabacher

Check all of the following that apply:

Open Session ☑   Electronically Recorded (taped) ☐
Executive (closed) Session ☐   Stenographic Record ☑
Televised ☑

TITLE OF HEARING:

"China's Maritime and other Geographic Threats"

SUBCOMMITTEE MEMBERS PRESENT:

Steve Stockman, TX; William Keating, MA; Alan S. Lowenthal, CA

NON-SUBCOMMITTEE MEMBERS PRESENT: *(Mark with an * if they are not members of full committee.)*

None.

HEARING WITNESSES: Same as meeting notice attached? Yes ☑ No ☐
(If "no", please list below and include title, agency, department, or organization.)

STATEMENTS FOR THE RECORD: *(List any statements submitted for the record.)*

QFR - Rep. Ted Poe

TIME SCHEDULED TO RECONVENE _____
or
TIME ADJOURNED _____*11:39*_____

Subcommittee Staff Director

50

Statement for the Record
Submitted by the Honorable Ted Poe

Chinese aggression in the South and East China Sea is alive and well. In February, a Chinese war ship targeted a Japanese destroyer and helicopter over a territorial dispute involving the Senkaku Islands. In May, a Vietnamese fishing boat was surrounded by Chinese boats and intentionally rammed. In June, 18 Chinese vessels were reportedly carrying out surveillance operations in Philippine territory, as Chine has sought to consolidate its control of the West Philippine Sea.

If China continues to operate like the bully of the Pacific, the security risks threaten to get out of hand. China's growing military capabilities and modernization has raised a lot of questions about their objectives and how they might pursue them. We also need to pay as much attention to civilian ships—China's small stick—as we do to big-stick platforms that dominate headlines. It's not hard to see how a minor dispute could turn into a catastrophic event.

The administration has talked a lot about a pivot to the Pacific in recent years. Over the past decade, our military has been consumed with the Middle East and Southwest Asia. The U.S. wants freedom of access to the South China Sea and we want to maintain regional peace and stability in Southeast Asia.

Enforcing global rules and norms while protecting our economic interests are also a top priority. A blue water navy allows us power projection and the ability to pursue free trade. The Chinese have the greatest capacity and more of a willingness to set norms and enforce its will. This is a deliberate strategy on their part.

Since at least 2007, we've seen Beijing increase its diplomatic and not-so-diplomatic actions to protect their interests. They've been more aggressive toward their neighbors, bullied commercial vessels and encroached on disputed territory. This has caused serious friction between China and its neighbors. No one country in the region can match the Chinese by themselves. Instead, we need a balancing effort among interested and like-minded parties. The Association of South East Asian Nations or ASEAN might be the best way to do this but it's no silver bullet. Unfortunately, if history is any guide, member countries have been too busy fighting amongst themselves.

We need to find a better way to curb the worst aspects of China's behavior while working with our friends and allies in the region to protect our mutual interests. I look forward to hearing from our witnesses.

Questions for the Record
Submitted by the Honorable Ted Poe
*To Peter Sandby-Thomas, Ph.D., Visiting Lecturer of Political Science, University
of Massachusetts Dartmouth*

QUESTION 1:

**Given the South China Sea's importance for shipping and China's reliance on trade, how
likely is it that China would start a military conflict in the area? Wouldn't this hurt
China's economy just as much as any other country's economy?**

Answer: As the question points out, the importance of the South China Sea for China's economy
would suggest that it is unlikely to start a military conflict in the area. However, such thinking
assumes that the initiation of military engagement would be solely based on rational calculations
and, though history has demonstrated that this is normally the case, it is not always so. Indeed, if
one looks at China's actions vis-à-vis Japan since the latter's nationalization of the 3 of the
Senkaku Islands in September 2012, it was long assumed that economic interdependence
between the two countries and likely negative economic effects of any dispute would likely deter
the outbreak of hostilities. The subsequent escalation of tensions since September 2012 was,
therefore, unanticipated and has resulted in economic damage. Notably, however, the damage
has been on both sides–something that would also be the case in the South China Sea–and yet the
situation shows no sign of abating. At this stage, there are two possible explanations for this. One
would be to conclude that the economic damage caused by the dispute is not yet significant
enough to prompt a change in strategy. Alternatively, it may be that the economic damage is
considered to be of lesser importance to other strategic goals. And if this second explanation is
valid, that would suggest that we cannot necessarily assume that China will not launch some
form of military engagement to achieve strategic control of the South China Sea.

Of course, it should be pointed out that, at this stage, China has given no direct indication that it
is prepared to use force to gain control of the South China Sea. It has made extravagant claims to
the area but, then again, so have a number of other countries in that region. The more disquieting
aspect is that China claims offer the potential to alter the existing status quo in a vital Sea Lane
of Communication and its intentions for doing so are unclear. The military option still looks
unlikely at this stage and the process

QUESTION 2:

What is your analysis of the U.S.'s current efforts to relieve tensions? What are we doing that works and does not work?

Answer: Unfortunately, I do not feel that I have sufficient expertise to comment directly on US efforts in this matter, other than stating that the US' commitment to ensuring a multilateral solution agreed upon by all the claimants represents the most efficacious outcome. Moreover, its military and naval presence in the area also seems to be necessary in preventing the escalation of military tension. Given the importance of this area for the US economy, it has clear grounds for exercising national interest and greater active involvement in any resolution, unlike the current disputes between China and Japan, and China and the Philippines.

Question for the Record
Submitted by the Honorable Ted Poe
To Perry Pickert, Ph.D., Retired Career Intelligence Officer

Question 1:

Do these acts of Chinese aggression threaten our national security interests?

Answer: The United States strategic interests as a Pacific power will not be directly impacted by the projected growth of Chinese naval power. The Chinese will need to acknowledge and support the basic rules concerning the freedom of the sea because they will need to use these rules to assert their status a great power. Their future access to 98% of high sea, its resources and the seabed depends on universal rules.

Problems will arise because China will take a bilateral approach to each of the territorial issues on their periphery. Starting with the Senkakus and stretching the bottom of the South China Sea the Chinese will take a patient approach, waiting for an opportunity to use their maximum asymmetric leverage to gain acceptance of a particular claim, no matter how dubious, by the weaker country. The risk of war with any of these countries is minimal. Since the United States is not party to any of these disputes, the Chinese do not consider US intervention as likely. The threshold for international action would be a "threat to international peace and security" under the UN Charter and the Chinese veto and even double veto would prevent Security Council action and maybe even consideration of the issues.

Thus the United States can anticipate years even decades of tempests in the China's teapots.

Chinese acquisition of longer range and highly lethal and accurate tactical missile system make these island disputes even more dangerous. The landmass of the vast majority of these disputed islands means they cannot be occupied and held by military force. The islands value really depends on the potential for exploiting the undersea resources in the surrounding waters. The expense of a single oil or gas platform runs into hundreds of millions of dollars – hardly a risk profile likely to attract investors.

The primary usefulness of these territorial confrontations is to demonstrate the expanding scope of China's new regional status as hegemon and kindle the fire Chinese nationalism to validate the legitimacy of the Chinese leadership.

US bilateral and multilateral diplomacy will only have marginal impact as it is the status quo on the ground and surrounding waters that matters. Bilateral military support for Japan and the ASEAN countries so they have the capability to independently provide continuous monitoring and quick reaction by air and sea to Chinese provocations is the most practical contribution the US can make.

Questions for the Record
Submitted by the Honorable Ted Poe
To Mr. Rick Fisher, Senior Fellow, Asian Military Affairs, International
Assessment and Strategy Center

Question 1:

How developed is China's navy? How does it compare to ours?

Answer: It is a pleasure to answer Congressman Poe's questions. The People's Liberation Army Navy (PLAN) is currently in an extended transition from assembling a balanced fleet necessary to support regional combat and support missions in the Asian theater, to acquiring the balanced capabilities needed to support significant global power projection. This transition may occur as early as the mid-to-later 2020s.

While modern PLAN ships may not be as capable as comparable ships in the U.S. Navy, the PLAN is improving and singular comparison is becoming less relevant, as in terms of a combined force, the PLAN is increasingly able to pose a credible threat to U.S. carrier battle groups operating in East Asia. While this combined capability is an early stage, during the week of 21 October 2013 the PLAN practiced combined submarine, surface ship and bomber exercises south of Japan's Sakashima Island Group, or east of Taiwan. This is not easy to do that far from shore bases and it marks significant achievement for the PLAN. When you add the unique PLA capability of long range anti-ship ballistic missiles and the new YJ-12 supersonic anti-ship missiles launched from bombers to this level of combined force, then it has to be said that the PLAN does have a growing capability for successfully attacking U.S. Navy forces in this theater.

Just a few observations: The PLAN is making non-nuclear submarines that are approaching the acoustic and tactical flexibility of the Russian *Kilo,* but with air independent propulsion (AIP). Chinese sources suggest that a new 200km range version of the HHQ-9 surface-to-air missile may soon enter service, which is approaching the capability of the U.S. SM-2 SAM. Longer range BMD naval SAMs are also to be expected. The J-15 carrier fighter that is entering service on the PLAN carrier *Liaoning* will be as capable as the U.S. Boeing F/A-18E/F once it is upgraded with an electronically scanned array radar, which may happed fairly soon. The U.S has a clear superiority in nuclear attack submarines, but the problem is that they are not sufficient in number to counter a surge of PLAN submarines, and still prosecute surface and land targets.

Question 2:

Out of all these acts of aggression, do any of them cross any red lines in your mind?

Answer: In terms of maintaining the credibility of U.S. alliance commitments in Asia, the year 2012 was a year of significant set-back. In April-May of 2012 China successfully bullied the Philippines from Scarborough Shoal in the South China Sea and then later in the year sent multiple Chinese Coast Guard ships into the territorial waters of the Senkaku Islands. This, unfortunately, has emboldened China to believe that it can increase pressures to push the Philippines and Japan out of areas that it either claims or occupies. In terms of the paramount U.S. interest in deterring conflict in Asia, we have allowed China to cross a red line, as having allowed "aggression" to go unanswered, we have only encouraged China to expand the scope of its aggression. We are not paying the price in 2013: Chinese harassment of the Philippine rusting ship "base" on Second Thomas Shoal and an increasing campaign of intimidation against Japan in the Senkakus.

The self-inflicted problem is that since the 1970s has been the consistent U.S. policy toward both regions to maintain strict neutrality regarding competing claims to territory in the South and East China Seas. Washington should have cast China's expansive claims to the South China Sea as a threat to regional peace since this claim was being formulated in the 1980s and affirmed in the 1990s. While former Secretary of State Hillary Clinton has tried to modify U.S. policy to object to the use of war to enforce claims, this policy has not been backed up by real responses to Chinese aggression. The right response to China's bullying in the last two years would have been to transfer ATACMS short range ballistic missiles to the Philippines and to offer them to Japan as well. Even if neither took up that option it still would have sent a clear message to China that the U.S. is quite willing to help check its aggression.

Æ

www.ingramcontent.com/pod-product-compliance
Lightning Source LLC
Chambersburg PA
CBHW080444290526
45791CB00008BA/2597